Our selection of the city's best p[...] eat, drink and experience:

Sights

Eating

Drinking

Entertainment

Shopping

These symbols give you the vital information for each listing:

- Telephone Numbers
- Opening Hours
- Parking
- Nonsmoking
- Internet Access
- Wi-Fi Access
- Vegetarian Selection
- English-Language Menu
- Family-Friendly
- Pet-Friendly
- Bus
- Ferry
- Metro
- Subway
- Tram
- Train

Find each listing quickly on maps for each neighbourhood:

Lonely Planet Pocket Guides are designed to get you straight to the heart of Venice.

Inside you'll find all the must-see sights, plus tips to make your visit to each one really memorable. We've split the city into easy-to-navigate neighbourhoods and provided clear maps so you'll find your way around with ease. Our expert authors have searched out the best of Venice: walks, food, nightlife and shopping, to name a few. Because you want to explore, our 'Local Life' pages will take you to some of the most exciting areas to experience the real Venice.

And of course you'll find all the practical tips you need for a smooth trip: itineraries for short visits, how to get around, and how much to tip the guy who serves you a drink at the end of a long day's exploration.

It's your guarantee of a really great experience.

Our Promise

You can trust our travel information because Lonely Planet authors visit the places we write about, each and every edition. We never accept freebies for positive coverage, so you can rely on us to tell it like it is.

QuickStart Guide 7

Explore Venice 21

The Best of Venice 149

Venice's Best Walks

Venice's Best...

Survival Guide 173

QuickStart Guide

Welcome to Venice

'Ooooooeeeee!' Gondoliers call out in narrow canals. With the world's highest density of Unesco-protected masterpieces, Venice will earn gasps from you too. Once you've seen palaces built on water, partied in costume like Casanova and eaten chorus lines of red-footed lagoon scallops, you'll greet every canal bend with anticipation.

Gondolas
RASTOS PHOTOGRAPHER/SHUTTERSTOCK ©

Venice Top Sights

Basilica di San Marco (p24)

East meets West in this architectural treasure.

S-F/SHUTTERSTOCK ©

Palazzo Ducale (p28)

The doge's magnificent gilded cage.

Peggy Guggenheim Collection (p52)

Peggy's avant-garde modernist collection.

HOWARD SANDLER/SHUTTERSTOCK ©

ANNA GUBAREVA/SHUTTERSTOCK ©

I Frari (p72)

A Gothic masterpiece full of treasure.

TATYANA ABRAMOVICH/SHUTTERSTOCK ©

Rialto Market (p74)

Venice's historic food market.

Gallerie dell'Accademia (p50)

A repository of Venetian masterpieces.

Scuola Grande di San Rocco (p70)

Tintoretto's masterpieces.

VVOE/SHUTTERSTOCK ©

RENATA SEDMAKOVA/ALAMY ©

FUNKYFOOD LONDON - PAUL WILLIAMS/ALAMY ©

Basilica di Santa Maria Assunta (p132)

The lagoon's oldest Byzantine basilica.

Venice Local Life

Local experiences and hidden gems to help you uncover the real city

To get to know Venice from the inside out, hit the *calli* (lanes) to find artisans' studios, *bacari* (hole-in-the-wall bars) and music venues for glimpses of Venetian life after hours and behind the scenes, and then visit the outer islands Venetians have called home for a millennium.

Cannaregio's Cicheti Circuit (p98)

☑ Creative seafood ☑ Venetian small plates

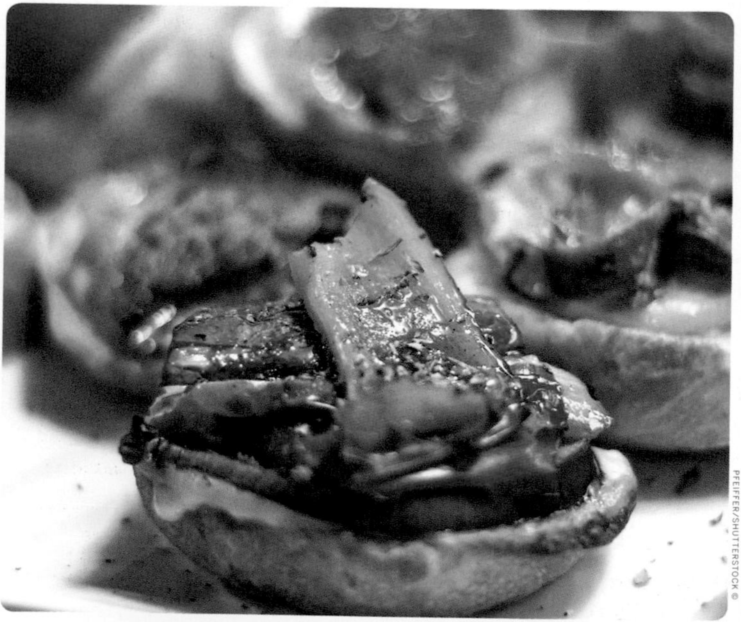

Happy Hour in Campo Santa Margherita (p54)

☑ *Spritz* cocktails ☑ Local wines

KOSTASTUDIO/SHUTTERSTOCK ©

Bars & Beaches on the Lido (p138)

☑ Beaches ☑ Alfresco entertainment

CLAUDIO DIVIZIA/SHUTTERSTOCK ©

Other great places to experience the city like a local:

Venice Day Planner

Day One

Begin your day on the Secret Itineraries tour of the **Palazzo Ducale** (p28), then break for espresso at the baroque counter of **Grancaffè Quadri** (p42) before the Byzantine blitz of golden mosaics inside the **Basilica di San Marco** (p24). Browse boutique-lined backstreets to **Museo Fortuny** (p36), the fashion house whose goddess-style gowns freed women from corsets.

Pause atop Ponte dell'Accademia for Grand Canal photo ops, then surrender to timeless drama inside **Gallerie dell'Accademia** (p50). Wander past **Squero di San Trovaso** (p63) to glimpse gondolas under construction and then bask in the reflected glory of Palladio's **Il Redentore** (p137) on a waterfront walk along the Zattere. Stop at tiny **Chiesa di San Sebastiano** (p58), packed with Veroneses, then hop between artisan boutiques along Calle Lunga San Barnaba before '*spritz* o'clock' (cocktail hour) in **Campo Santa Margherita** (p54).

Leap back into the 1700s at nearby **Scuola Grande dei Carmini** (p59), the evocative setting for costumed classical concerts by **Musica in Maschera** (p65). Alternatively, end the night on a saxy note at modern veteran **Venice Jazz Club** (p64).

Day Two

Kick off day two with a crash course in lagoon delicacies at the produce-packed **Rialto Market** (p74), side-stepping it to **Drogheria Mascari** (p90) for gourmet pantry fillers and regional wines, and to **All'Arco** (p82) for a cheeky morning *prosecco* (sparkling wine). Boutiques and artisan studios punctuate your way to Campo San Rocco, home to Gothic show-off **I Frari** (p72) and its sunny Titian altarpiece. Once admired, slip into **Scuola Grande di San Rocco** (p70) for prime-time-drama Tintorettos.

Explore the modern art that caused uproars and defined the 20th century at the **Peggy Guggenheim Collection** (p52), and contrast it with works that push contemporary buttons at **Punta della Dogana** (p58). Duck into Baldassare Longhena's domed **Basilica di Santa Maria della Salute** (p58) for blushing Titians and legendary curative powers, then cross the Grand Canal on Venice's only wooden bridge, Ponte dell'Accademia.

The hottest ticket in town during opera season is at **La Fenice** (p44), but classical-music fans shouldn't miss Vivaldi played with contemporary verve by **Interpreti Veneziani** (p33).

Short on time?
We've arranged Venice's must-sees into these day-by-day itineraries to make sure you see the very best of the city in the time you have available.

Day Three

Stroll Riva degli Schiavoni for views across the lagoon to Palladio's **Basilica di San Giorgio Maggiore** (p130). See how Carpaccio's sprightly saints light up a room at **Scuola Dalmata di San Giorgio degli Schiavoni** (p116), then seek out Castello's hidden wonder: **Chiesa di San Francesco della Vigna** (p116). Get stared down by statues atop **Ospedaletto** (p126) on your way to Gothic **Zanipolo** (p116), home to 25 marble doges.

Dip into pretty, Renaissance **Chiesa di Santa Maria dei Miracoli** (p102), a polychrome marble miracle made from the Basilica di San Marco's leftovers, before wandering serene *fondamente* (canal banks) past Moorish statues ringing Campo dei Mori to reach **Chiesa della Madonna dell'Orto** (p102), the Gothic church Tintoretto pimped with masterpieces. Then tour the **Ghetto's synagogues** (p96) until Venice's happiest hours beckon across the bridge at **Timon** (p99).

Take a romantic gondola ride through the long canals of **Cannaregio** (p94), seemingly purpose-built to maximise moonlight.

Day Four

Make your lagoon getaway on a *vaporetto* (small passenger ferry) bound for green-and-gold Torcello and technicolour Burano. Follow the sheep trail to Torcello's Byzantine **Basilica di Santa Maria Assunta** (p132), where the apse's golden Madonna calmly stares down the blue devils opposite. Catch the boat back to Burano to admire extreme home-design colour schemes and handmade lace at **Museo del Merletto** (p141).

Take in the fiery passions of glass artisans at Murano's legendary *fornaci* (furnaces), and see their finest moments showcased at the fabulously renovated **Museo del Vetro** (p135). After Murano showrooms close, hop the *vaporetto* to Giudecca for some spa-loving at the **JW Marriott Spa** (p147) and unbeatable views of San Marco glittering across glassy waters.

Celebrate your triumphant tour of the lagoon with a *prosecco* toast and tango across Piazza San Marco at time-warped **Caffè Florian** (p33); repeat these last steps as necessary.

Need to Know

For more information, see Survival Guide (p173)

Currency
Euro (€)

Language
Italian and Venetian (dialect)

Visas
Not required for EU citizens. Nationals of Australia, Brazil, Canada, Japan, New Zealand and the USA do not need visas for visits of up to 90 days.

Money
ATMs are widely available and credit cards accepted at most hotels, B&Bs and shops. To change money you'll need to present your ID.

Mobile Phones
GSM and tri-band phones can be used in Italy with a local SIM card.

Time
GMT/UTC plus one hour during winter; GMT/UTC plus two hours during summer daylight saving.

Tipping
Optional 10% for good service at restaurants where not included in the bill; at least €2 per bag or night, for porter, maid or room service; optional for gondolas and water taxis; leave spare change for prompt service at bar and cafe counters.

1 Before You Go

Your Daily Budget

Budget: Less than €120

- Dorm bed: €35–60
- *Cicheti* (bar snacks) at All'Arco: €5–15
- *Spritz* (*prosecco* cocktail): €2.50–4

Midrange: €120–250

- B&B: €70–180
- Civic Museum Pass: €24
- Midrange dinner: €35–40

Top End: More than €250

- Boutique hotel: €200-plus
- Gondola ride: €80
- Top-end dinner: €50–60

Useful Websites

- **Lonely Planet** (www.lonelyplanet.com/venice) Expert travel advice.
- **Venice Comune** (www.comune.venezia.it) City of Venice official site with essential info, including high-water alerts.
- **VeneziaUnica** (www.veneziaunica.it) The main tourism portal with online ticketing for public transport and tourist cards.

Advance Planning

Two months before Book high-season accommodation and tickets to La Fenice, Venice Film Festival premieres and Biennale openings.

Three weeks before Check special-event calendars at www.veneziadavivere.com, and reserve boat trips.

One week before Make restaurant reservations for a big night out; skip the queues by booking tickets to major attractions, exhibitions and events online at www.veneziaunica.it.

2 Arriving in Venice

Most people arrive in Venice by train, plane and, more controversially, cruise ship. There is a long-distance bus service to the city and it is also possible to drive to Venice, though you have to park at the western end of the city and then walk or take a *vaporetto* (small passenger ferry).

Flights, tours and rail tickets can be booked online at lonelyplanet.com/bookings.

Marco Polo Airport

▶ **Marco Polo Airport** (flight information 041 260 92 60; www.veniceairport.it; Via Galileo Gallilei 30/1, Tessera) is Venice's main international airport and is located in Tessera, 12km east of Mestre.

▶ Inside the terminal you'll find ticket offices for water taxis and **Alilaguna water bus transfers** (041 240 17 01; www.alilaguna.it; airport transfer one-way €15), and a **Vènezia Unica tourist office** (041 24 24; www.veneziaunica.it; Arrivals Hall; 8.30am-7pm) where you can pick-up pre-ordered travel cards and a map.

Stazione Venezia Santa Lucia

▶ Regional and international trains run frequently to Venice's Santa Lucia train station (www.veneziasantalucia.it; Fondamenta Santa Lucia, Cannaregio), appearing on signs as Ferrovia within Venice. The station has a helpful tourist office (041 24 24; www.veneziaunica.it; 7am-9pm; Ferrovia) opposite platform 3 where you can obtain a map and buy *vaporetto* tickets.

▶ *Vaporetti* (Azienda del Consorzio Trasporti Veneziano; 041 272 21 11; www.actv.it) connect Santa Lucia train station with all parts of Venice. There is also a water-taxi rank just out front.

3 Getting Around

Walking is the most scenic and often easiest way to get around Venice – and it's free. The other way to navigate this city on the water is by boat, and there are plenty of boating options. Cars and bicycles can be used on the Lido.

Vaporetto

These small passenger ferries are Venice's main public transport – note the line and direction of travel at the dock to make sure you catch the right boat. Single rides cost €7.50; for frequent use, get a timed pass for unlimited travel within a set period (1/2/3/7-day passes cost €20/30/40/60).

Gondola

Not mere transport but an adventure – and the best way to slip into Venice's smaller canals. Daytime rates run to €80 for 30 minutes (six passengers maximum) or €100 for 35 minutes from 7pm to 8am, not including songs or tips.

Water Taxi

The only door-to-door option, but fares are steep at €15 plus €2 per minute, plus surcharges for night-time, luggage, large groups and hotel services. Book ahead.

Traghetto

Locals use this daytime public gondola service (€2) to cross the Grand Canal between bridges.

Bicycle

Only allowed on the Lido, where bike hire is available and affordable (€9 per day).

Car

No cars are allowed in Venice beyond Piazzale Roma, where parking starts at €15 per day. Cars can be used on the Lido.

Venice Neighbourhoods

San Polo & Santa Croce (p68)
Treasure hunts in these side-by-side *sestieri* uncover priceless Titians, courtesan couture, scientific wonders and culinary gems.

Top Sights

- Scuola Grande di San Rocco
- I Frari
- Rialto Market

Dorsoduro & the Accademia (p48)
Venice's historic artists' quarter is packed with controversial artworks, hallowed architecture and marathon happy hours.

Top Sights

- Gallerie dell'Accademia
- Peggy Guggenheim Collection

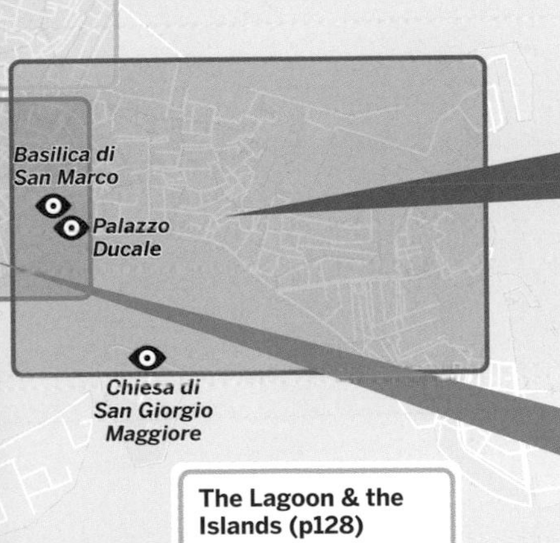

Cannaregio & the Ghetto (p94)
Follow serene canalbanks for bargain *cicheti* (Venetian tapas), priceless Tintorettos and a tiny island with a big history.

Top Sights

Campo del Ghetto Nuovo & the Ghetto

Castello (p112)
Between Arsenale shipyards and Biennale pavilions, you can dine like a doge, drink like a sailor and stroll waterfront promenades.

San Marco & Palazzo Ducale (p22)
A downtown like no other: gondola traffic, acres of golden mosaics and legendary escapes from a pink Gothic prison.

Top Sights

Basilica di San Marco

Palazzo Ducale

The Lagoon & the Islands (p128)

Top Sights

Basilica di Santa Maria Assunta

Chiesa di San Giorgio Maggiore

Explore Venice

Gondolas on the Grand Canal
OLENA Z/SHUTTERSTOCK ©

Explore

San Marco & Palazzo Ducale

So many world-class attractions are packed into San Marco, some visitors never leave – and others are reluctant to visit, fearing crowds. But why miss the pleasures of the Basilica di San Marco, Palazzo Ducale, Museo Correr and jewel-box La Fenice? Judge for yourself whether they earn their reputations – but don't stop there. The backstreets are packed with galleries, boutiques and bars.

The Sights in a Day

Everything started here in the 9th century, when Doge Partecipazio built his palace on the *rivo alto* (high bank). Join the chorus of gasps from the crowds as you enter the **Basilica di San Marco** (p24) to discover angels dancing across golden mosaic domes. With the palace, prison, mint and library crowding around Piazza San Marco, you could spend days here, so choose carefully, prioritising either **Palazzo Ducale** (pictured left; p28) or the **Museo Correr** (p36).

Nab a quick lunch at **Osteria da Carla** (p42), then hit the backstreets between Piazza San Marco and the Ponte dell'Accademia to search out Venetian artists handcrafting handbags, textiles, travel journals and glass. Detour for history-making fashion and modern art at **Museo Fortuny** (p36).

Savour sunset cocktails at **L'Ombra del Leoni** (p43) or swish **Bar Longhi** (p42) before donning your best threads for a red-carpet night at **La Fenice** (p44) or the damask-lined dining room at **Ristorante Quadri** (p40). Indulge in a romantic nightcap at **Caffè Florian** (p33) and watch the Moors strike midnight atop the **Torre dell'Orologio** (p37), heralding the end of another day in the charmed life of this floating city.

For a local's day in San Marco, see p32.

Top Sights

Local Life

Best of Venice

Architecture

Museums

Getting There

Vaporetto Line 1 serves stops on the Grand Canal; line 2 is faster and stops at Rialto, San Samuele and San Marco Giardinetti.

Traghetto A gondola ferry crosses the Grand Canal from Santa Maria del Giglio.

Walk Follow yellow-signed shortcuts from Rialto through shop-lined Marzarie to Piazza San Marco. It's often quicker than the *vaporetto*.

Top Sights
Basilica di San Marco

In a city packed with architectural wonders, none beats St Mark's for sheer spectacle and bombastic exuberance. In AD 828, wily Venetian merchants allegedly smuggled St Mark's corpse out of Egypt in a barrel of pork fat to avoid inspection by Muslim authorities. Venice built a basilica around its stolen saint in keeping with its own sense of supreme self-importance.

St Mark's Basilica

Map p34, H3

041 270 83 11

www.basilicasanmarco.it

Piazza San Marco

9.45am-5pm Mon-Sat, 2-5pm Sun, to 4pm Sun winter

San Marco

Dome mosaics

Construction

Church authorities in Rome took a dim view of Venice's tendency to glorify itself and God in the same breath, but the city defiantly created a private chapel for their doge that outshone Venice's official cathedral (the Basilica di San Pietro in Castello) in every conceivable way. After the original St Mark's was burned down during an uprising, Venice rebuilt the basilica two more times (mislaying and rediscovering the saint's body along the way). The current incarnation was completed in 1094, reflecting the city's cosmopolitan image, with Byzantine domes, a Greek cross layout and walls clad in marbles looted from Syria, Egypt and Palestine.

Facade

The front of St Mark's ripples and crests like a wave, its five niched portals capped with shimmering mosaics and frothy stonework arches. It's especially resplendent just before sunset, when the sun's dying rays set the golden mosaics ablaze. Grand entrances are made through the central portal, under an ornate triple arch featuring Egyptian purple porphyry columns and intricate 13th- to 14th-century stone reliefs. The oldest mosaic on the facade, dating from 1270, is in the lunette above the far-left portal, depicting St Mark's stolen body arriving at the basilica. The theme is echoed in three of the other lunettes, including the 1660 mosaics above the second portal from the right, showing turbaned officials recoiling from the hamper of pork fat containing the sainted corpse.

Dome Mosaics

Blinking is natural upon your first glimpse of the basilica's 8500 sq metres of glittering mosaics, many made with 24-carat gold leaf fused onto

☑ Top Tips

- There's no charge to enter the church and wander around the roped-off central circuit, although you'll need to dress modestly (ie knees and shoulders covered) and leave large bags around the corner at the **Ateneo San Basso Left Luggage Office** (Piazza San Marco; free for maximum 1hr; ⏲9.30am-5pm).
- Between mid-September and October, the diocese offers free **guided tours** (☎041 241 38 17; www.basilicasanmarco.it; ⏲11.30am Mon-Sat mid-Sep–Oct) explaining the theological messages in the mosaics. They're given in different languages on different days; check online for details.

Take a Break

Bask in the afterglow of the basilica's golden magnificence within the jewellery-box interior of Caffè Florian (p33).

the back of the glass to represent divine light. Just inside the narthex (vestibule) glitter the basilica's oldest mosaics, **Apostles with the Madonna**, standing sentry by the main door for more than 950 years. The atrium's medieval **Dome of Genesis** depicts the separation of sky and water with surprisingly abstract motifs, anticipating modern art by 650 years.

Inside the church proper, three golden domes vie for your attention. The images are intended to be read from the altar end to the entry, so the **Cupola of the Prophets** shimmers above the main altar, while the **Last Judgment** is depicted in the vault above the entrance (and best seen from the museum). The dome nearest the door is the **Pentecost Cupola**, showing the Holy Spirit represented by a dove shooting tongues of flame onto the heads of the surrounding saints. In the central 13th-century **Ascension Cupola**, angels swirl around the central figure of Christ hovering among the stars. Scenes from St Mark's life unfold around the main altar, which houses the saint's simple stone **sarcophagus**.

Pala d'Oro

Tucked behind the main **altar** (admission €2), this stupendous golden screen is studded with 2000 emeralds, amethysts, sapphires, rubies, pearls and other gemstones. But the most priceless treasures here are biblical

Basilica di San Marco

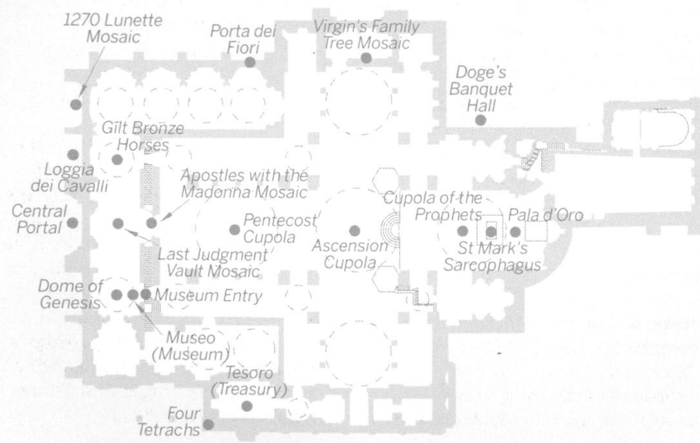

figures in vibrant cloisonné, begun in Constantinople in AD 976 and elaborated by Venetian goldsmiths in 1209. The enamelled saints have wild, unkempt beards and wide eyes fixed on Jesus, who glances sideways at a studious St Mark as Mary throws up her hands in wonder – an understandable reaction to such a captivating scene.

Treasury

Holy bones and booty from the Crusades fill the **Tesoro** (treasury; admission €3), including a 4th-century rock-crystal lamp, a 10th-century rock-crystal ewer with winged feet made for Fatimid Caliph al-'Aziz-billah, and an exquisite enamelled 10th-century Byzantine chalice. Don't miss the bejewelled 12th-century Archangel Michael icon, featuring tiny, feisty enamelled saints that look ready to break free of their golden setting and mount a miniature attack on evil. In a separate room, velvet-padded boxes preserve the remains of sainted doges alongside the usual assortment of credulity-challenging relics: St Roch's femur, the arm St George used to slay the dragon and even a lock of the Madonna's hair.

Museum

Accessed by a narrow staircase leading up from the basilica's atrium, the **Museo di San Marco** (Basilica di San Marco; adult/reduced €5/2.50; 9.45am-4.45pm; San Marco) transports visitors to the level of the church's rear mosaics and out onto the **Loggia dei Cavalli**, the terrace above the main facade. The four magnificent bronze horses positioned here are actually reproductions of the precious 2nd-century originals, plundered from Constantinople's hippodrome, displayed inside.

Pala d'Oro

Architecture buffs will revel in the beautifully rendered drawings and scale models of the basilica. In the displays of 13th- to 16th-century mosaic fragments, the Prophet Abraham is all ears and raised eyebrows, as though scandalised by Venetian gossip. A corridor leads into a section of the Palazzo Ducale containing the **doge's banquet hall**, where dignitaries wined and dined among lithe stucco figures of *Music*, *Poetry* and *Peace*.

Top Sights
Palazzo Ducale

Don't be fooled by its genteel Gothic elegance: behind that lacy, pink-and-white-patterned facade, the doge's palace shows serious muscle and a steely will to survive. The seat of Venice's government for over seven centuries, this powerhouse stood the test of storms, crashes and conspiracies – only to be outwitted by Casanova, the notorious seducer who escaped from the attic prison.

Map p34, H4

041 271 59 11

www.palazzoducale.visitmuve.it

Piazzetta San Marco 1

adult/reduced incl Museo Correr €19/12

8.30am-7pm Apr-Oct, to 5.30pm Nov-Mar

San Zaccaria

Palazzo Ducale courtyard with Scala dei Giganti

Architecture

After fire gutted the original palace in 1577, Antonio da Ponte restored its Gothic grandeur. The white Istrian stone and Veronese pink marble palace caps a graceful colonnade with medieval capitals depicting key Venetian guilds.

Courtyard

Entering through the colonnaded courtyard you'll spot Sansovino's brawny statues of *Apollo* and *Neptune* flanking Antonio Rizzo's **Scala dei Giganti** (Giants' Staircase). Recent restorations have preserved charming cherubim propping up the pillars, though slippery incised-marble steps remain off-limits. Just off the courtyard in the wing facing the square is the **Museo dell'Opera**, displaying a collection of stone columns and capitals from previous incarnations of the building.

Doge's Apartments

The doge's suite of private rooms take up a large chunk of the 1st floor above the loggia. This space is now used for temporary art exhibitions, which are tickcted separately (around €10 extra). The doge lived like a prisoner in his gilded suite in the palace, which he could not leave without permission. Still, consider the real estate: a terrace garden with private entry to the basilica, and a dozen salons with splendidly restored marble fireplaces carved by Tullio and Antonio Lombardo. The most intriguing room is the **Sala dello Scudo** (Shield Room), covered with world maps that reveal the extent of Venetian power (and the limits of its cartographers) c 1483 and 1762.

Sala delle Quattro Porte

From the loggia level, climb Sansovino's 24-carat gilt stuccowork **Scala d'Oro** (Golden Staircase) and emerge into rooms covered with gorgeous propaganda. In Palladio-designed **Sala**

☑ Top Tips

- ▶ Tickets (valid for three months) include the Museo Correr (p36) but it's worth paying an extra €5 for a Museum Pass, which gives access to several other high-profile civic museums.
- ▶ The last admission is one hour prior to closing.
- ▶ Don't leave your run until too late in the day, as some parts of the palace, such as the prisons, may close early.

Take a Break

Call into the humble but excellent **Pasticceria da Bonifacio** (041 522 75 07; Calle dei Albanesi 4237; pastries €1.10-2; 7.30am-6.30pm Fri-Wed; San Zaccaria) for a coffee, pastry or *spritz*.

delle Quattro Porte (Hall of the Four Doors), ambassadors awaited ducal audiences under a lavish display of Venice's virtues by Giovanni Cambi. Other convincing shows of Venetian superiority include Titian's 1576 *Doge Antonio Grimani Kneeling Before Faith* amid approving cherubim and Tiepolo's 1740s *Venice Receiving Gifts of the Sea from Neptune,* where Venice is a gorgeous blonde casually leaning on a lion.

Anticollegio

Delegations waited in the **Anticollegio** (Council Antechamber), where Tintoretto drew parallels between Roman gods and Venetian government: *Mercury and the Three Graces* reward Venice's industriousness with beauty, and *Minerva Dismissing Mars* is a Venetian triumph of savvy over brute force. The recently restored ceiling is Veronese's 1577 *Venice Distributing Honours,* while on the walls is a vivid reminder of diplomatic behaviour to avoid: Veronese's *Rape of Europe.*

Collegio & Sala del Senato

Few were granted an audience in the Palladio-designed **Collegio** (Council Chamber), where Veronese's 1575–78 *Virtues of the Republic* ceiling shows Venice as a bewitching blonde waving her sceptre like a wand over Justice and Peace. Father-son team Jacopo and Domenico Tintoretto attempt similar flattery, showing Venice keeping company with Apollo, Mars and Mercury in their *Triumph of Venice* ceiling for the **Sala del Senato** (Senate Chamber).

Sala Consiglio dei Dieci

Government cover-ups were never so appealing as in the **Sala Consiglio dei Dieci** (Chamber of the Council of Ten), where plots were hatched under Veronese's *Juno Bestowing her Gifts on Venice.* Over the slot where anonymous treason accusations were slipped into the **Sala della Bussola** (Compass Room) is his *St Mark in Glory* ceiling.

Sala del Maggior Consiglio

The grandest room on the 1st floor is the cavernous 1419 **Sala del Maggior Consiglio** (Grand Council Chamber). The doge's throne once stood in front of the staggering 22m-by-7m *Paradise* backdrop (by Tintoretto's son, Domenico) where heaven is crammed with 500 prominent Venetians, including several Tintoretto patrons. Veronese's political posturing is more elegant in his oval *Apotheosis of Venice* ceiling, where gods marvel at Venice's coronation by angels.

Secret Itineraries Tours

Further rooms can be visited on this fascinating 75-minute **tour** (☎041 4273 0892; adult/reduced €20/14; ⌚in English 9.55am, 10.45am & 11.35am, in Italian 9.30am & 11.10am, in French 10.20am & noon). It takes in the cells known as **Pozzi** (wells) and the **Council of Ten Secret Headquarters**. Beyond this ominous office suite, the **Chancellery** is lined with drawers of top-secret files, including reports by Venice's spy network. Upstairs lie the **Piombi** (Leads), the attic where Casanova was held in 1756. As described in his memoirs, he made an ingenious escape through the roof.

Palazzo Ducale

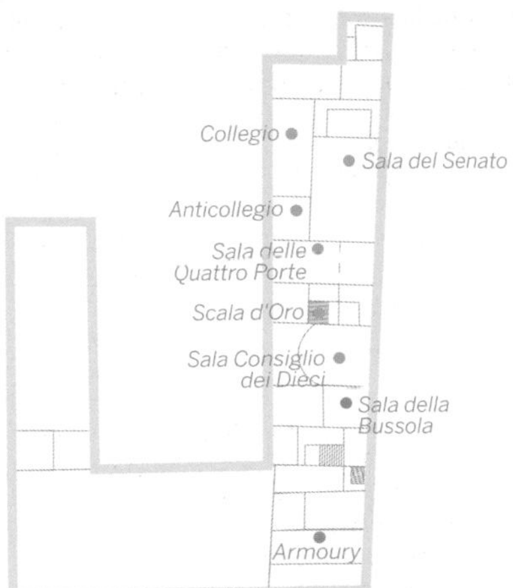

Level 2

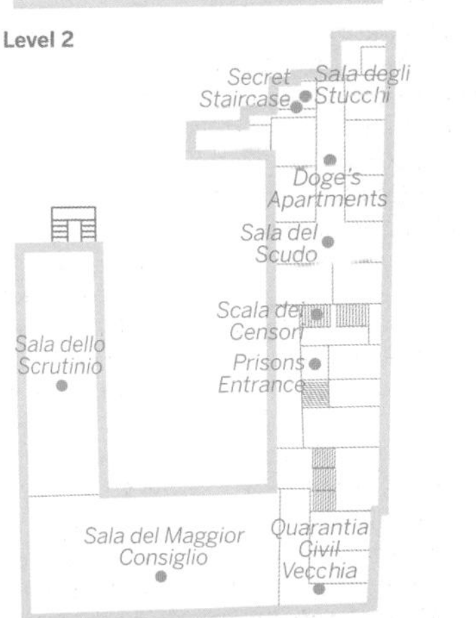

Level 1

Local Life
Music in San Marco

Once Venice's dominion over the high seas ended, it discovered the power of high Cs, hiring as San Marco choirmaster Claudio Monteverdi, the father of modern opera, and bringing on baroque with Antonio Vivaldi. Today, MP3s still can't compare to Venice's live-music offerings. While Teatro La Fenice is the obvious draw for opera lovers, try these other music destinations to immerse yourself in a Venetian soundtrack.

❶ Tarantella at Caffè Lavena

Opera composer Richard Wagner had the right idea: when Venice leaves you weak in the knees, get a pick-me-up at **Lavena** (☎041 522 40 70; www.lavena.it; Piazza San Marco 133/134; ⌚9.30am-11pm; ⛴San Marco). An espresso at Lavena's mirrored bar is a baroque bargain – try to ignore the politically incorrect antique 'Moor's head' chandeliers. Spring for piazza seating to savour *caffè corretto* (coffee

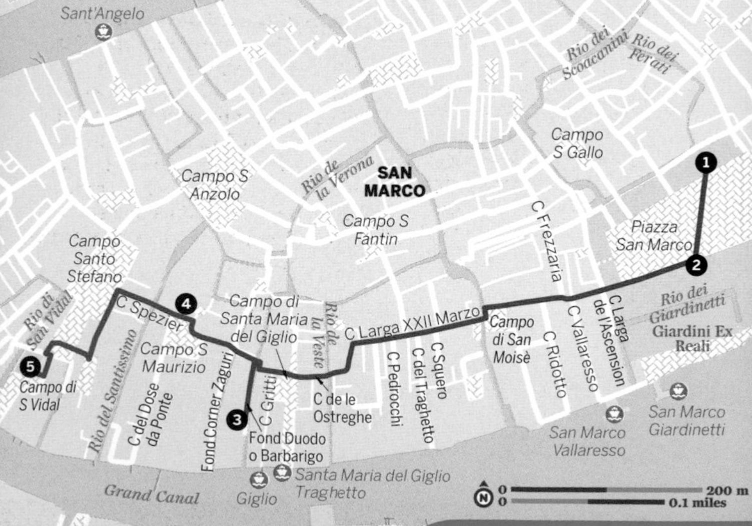

'corrected' with liquor) accompanied by Lavena's nimble violinists.

2 Tango at Caffè Florian

Caffè Florian (☎041 520 56 41; www.caffeflorian.com; Piazza San Marco 57; ⌚9am-11pm; ⛴San Marco) maintains rituals established c 1720: white-jacketed waiters serve cappuccino on silver trays, and the orchestra strikes up as sunsets illuminate San Marco's mosaics. Piazza seating during concerts costs €6 extra, but dreamy-eyed romantics hardly notice. Among Italy's first bars to welcome women and revolutionaries, Florian's radical-chic reputation persists with its art installations.

3 Arias at Musica a Palazzo

Hang onto your *prosecco:* it's always high drama in the historic salons of **Musica a Palazzo** (☎340 971 72 72; www.musicapalazzo.com; Palazzo Barbarigo Minotto, Fondamenta Duodo o Barbarigo 2504; ticket incl beverage €85; ⌚from 8pm; ⛴Giglio). The beautiful Venetian baroque palace overlooking the Grand Canal provides a unique, intimate setting as the audience follows the action from hall to hall, surrounded by authentic artworks and furnishings.

4 History at Museo della Musica

Housed in the restored neoclassical Chiesa di San Maurizio, **Museo della Musica** (☎041 241 18 40; www.museodellamusica.com; Campo San Maurizio 2603; admission free; ⌚9.30am-7pm; ⛴Giglio) presents a collection of rare 17th- to 20th-century instruments, accompanied by informative panels on the life and times of Venice's Antonio Vivaldi. The museum is funded by Interpreti Veneziani.

5 Baroque Bravado at Interpreti Veneziani

Everything you've heard of Vivaldi from weddings and mobile ringtones is proved fantastically wrong by **Interpreti Veneziani** (☎041 277 05 61; www.interpretiveneziani.com; Chiesa San Vidal, Campo di San Vidal 2862; adult/reduced €29/24; ⌚performances 8.30pm; ⛴Accademia), who play Vivaldi on 18th-century instruments as a soundtrack for living in this city of intrigue – you'll never listen to *The Four Seasons* again without hearing summer storms erupting over the lagoon, or snow-muffled footsteps hurrying over footbridges in winter's-night intrigues.

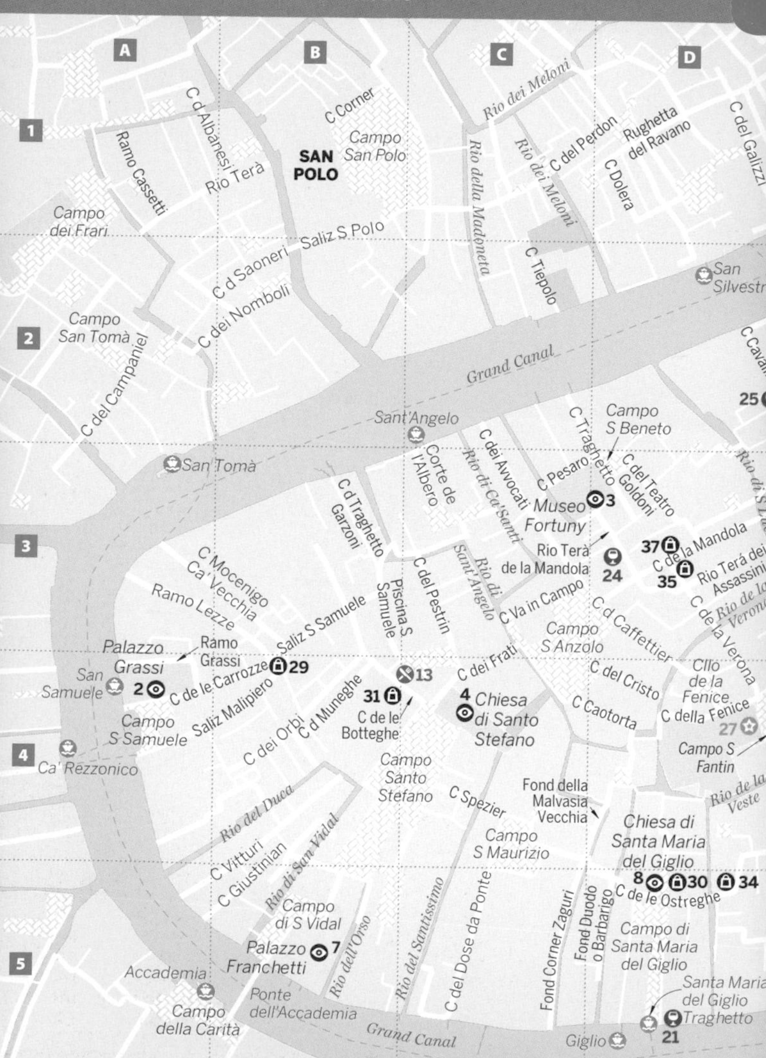

A
B
C
D
1
2
3
4
5
SAN POLO
Campo San Polo
C Corner
C d'Albanesi
Ramo Cassetti
Rio Terà
Campo dei Frari
Saliz S Polo
C d Saoneri
C dei Nomboli
Campo San Tomà
C del Campaniel
Rio dei Meloni
Rio della Madoneta
C del Perdon
Rughetta del Ravano
C Dolera
C del Galizzi
C Tiepolo
San Silvestr
Grand Canal
C Cavall
25
Sant'Angelo
San Tomà
Campo S Beneto
C Traghetto
C dei Avvocati
Rio di Ca'Santi
Corte de l'Albero
C d Traghetto Garzoni
C Pesaro
C del Teatro Goldoni
Museo Fortuny
3
Rio Terà de la Mandola
24
37
35
C de la Mandola
Rio Terà dei Assassini
Rio di S Luca
C Mocenigo Ca' Vecchia
Ramo Lezze
Saliz S Samuele
Piscina S Samuele
C del Pestrin
Rio di Sant'Angelo
C Va in Campo
Campo S Anzolo
C d Caffettier
Rio de la Verona
C de la Verona
Palazzo Grassi
Ramo Grassi
San Samuele
2
C de le Carrozze
29
Saliz Malipiero
31
13
C de le Botteghe
C d Muneghe
C dei Frati
4
Chiesa di Santo Stefano
C del Cristo
Cllo de la Fenice
C della Fenice
C Caotorta
27
Campo S Samuele
C dei Orbi
Ca' Rezzonico
Campo Santo Stefano
Campo S Fantin
C Spezier
Fond della Malvasia Vecchia
Rio de la Veste
Rio del Duca
Chiesa di Santa Maria del Giglio
Campo S Maurizio
C Vitturi
C Giustinian
Rio di San Vidal
8
30
34
C de le Ostreghe
Campo di S Vidal
Rio del Santissimo
C del Dose da Ponte
Fond Corner Zaguri
Fond Duodo o Barbarigo
Campo di Santa Maria del Giglio
Palazzo Franchetti
7
Rio dell'Orso
Accademia
Campo della Carità
Ponte dell'Accademia
Grand Canal
Santa Maria del Giglio Traghetto
21
Giglio

For reviews see

Top Sights	p24
Sights	p36
Eating	p40
Drinking	p42
Entertainment	p44
Shopping	p45

Sights

Museo Correr

MUSEUM

1 Map p34, F4

Napoleon bowled down an ancient church to build his royal digs over Piazza San Marco and then filled them with the riches of the doges while taking some of Venice's finest heirlooms to France as trophies. When Austria set up shop the Empress Sissi remodelled the palace, adding ceiling frescoes, silk cladding and brocade curtains. It's now open to the public and full of many of Venice's reclaimed treasures, including ancient maps, statues, cameos and four centuries of artistic masterpieces. (041 240 52 11; www.correr.visitmuve.it; Piazza San Marco 52; adult/reduced incl Palazzo Ducale €19/12, with Museum Pass free; 10am-7pm Apr-Oct, to 5pm Nov-Mar; San Marco)

Local Life

See Venice like a Venetian

Throughout San Marco you'll be tripping over iPhone touting tourists. Everyone, it seems, wants to capture the perfect Venetian scene. Getty photojournalist and Venetian, Marco Secchi, will show you how during an in-depth **photo tour** (041 963 73 74; www.venicephototour.com; 2/3/6-hr walking tours for up to 4 people €210/300/600) exploring the secret corners of the city. In particular, you'll learn how to capture the nuances of light and how to frame that masterpiece for the mantle. He can work with all types of camera, tailor tours to personal interests and arrange photography tours of the lagoon.

Palazzo Grassi

GALLERY

2 Map p34, A4

Grand Canal gondola riders gasp at first glimpse of massive sculptures by contemporary artists docked in front of Giorgio Masari's neoclassical palace (built 1748–72). French billionaire François Pinault's provocative art collection overflows Palazzo Grassi, while clever curation and shameless art-star name-dropping are the hallmarks of rotating temporary exhibits. Still, despite the artistic glamour, Tadao Ando's creatively repurposed interior architecture steals the show. (041 200 10 57; www.palazzograssi.it; Campo San Samuele 3231; adult/reduced incl Punta della Dogana €18/15; 10am-7pm Wed-Mon mid-Apr–Nov; San Samuele)

Museo Fortuny

MUSEUM

3 Map p34, D3

Find design inspiration at the palatial home-studio of art nouveau designer Mariano Fortuny y Madrazo (1871–1949), whose shockingly uncorseted Delphi goddess frocks set the standard for bohemian chic. First-floor salon walls are eclectic mood boards: Fortuny fashions and Isfahan tapestries, family portraits and

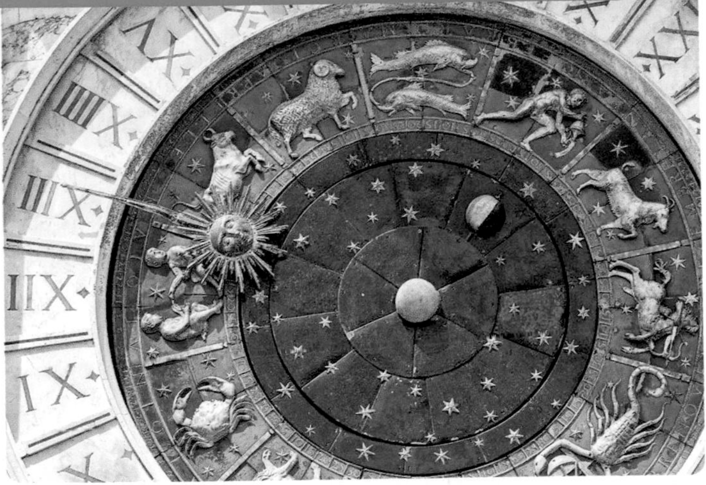

Torre dell'Orologio

artfully peeling plaster. Interesting temporary exhibitions spread from the basement to the attic, the best of which use the general ambience of grand decay to great effect. (☎041 520 09 95; www.fortuny.visitmuve.it; Campo San Beneto 3958; adult/reduced €12/10; ⌚10am-6pm Wed-Mon; ⛴Sant'Angelo)

Chiesa di Santo Stefano — CHURCH

4 Map p34, C4

The free-standing bell tower, visible from the square behind, leans disconcertingly, but this brick Gothic church has stood tall since the 13th century. Credit for shipshape splendour goes to Bartolomeo Bon for the marble entry portal and to Venetian shipbuilders, who constructed the vast wooden *carena di nave* (ship's keel) ceiling that resembles an upturned Noah's Ark. (☎041 522 50 61; www.chorusvenezia.org; Campo Santo Stefano; museum €4, with Chorus Pass free; ⌚10.30am-4.30pm Mon-Sat; ⛴Sant'Angelo)

Torre dell'Orologio — LANDMARK

5 Map p34, G3

The two hardest-working men in Venice stand duty on a rooftop around the clock, and wear no pants. No need to file workers' complaints: the 'Do Mori' (Two Moors) exposed to the elements atop the Torre dell'Orologio are made of bronze, and their bell-hammering mechanism runs like, well, clockwork. Below the Moors, Venice's gold-leafed, 15th-century timepiece tracks lunar phases. Visits are by guided tour; bookings essential. (Clock Tower; 041 4273 0892; www.museicivicivenezianі.it; Piazza San Marco; adult/reduced €12/7; tours by appointment; San Marco)

Campanile

TOWER

6 Map p34, G4

The basilica's 99m-tall bell tower has been rebuilt twice since its initial construction in AD 888. Galileo Galilei tested his telescope here in 1609, but modern-day visitors head to the top for 360-degree lagoon views and close encounters with the Marangona, the booming bronze bell that originally signalled the start and end of the working day for the craftsmen *(marangoni)* at the Arsenale shipyards. Today it rings twice a day, at noon and midnight. (Bell Tower; www.basilicasanmarco.it; Piazza San Marco; adult/reduced €8/4; 8.30am-9.30pm summer, 9.30am-5.30pm winter, last entry 45min prior; San Marco)

Palazzo Franchetti

PALACE

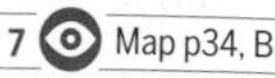

7 Map p34, B5

This 16th-century *palazzo* passed through the hands of various Venetian families before Archduke Frederik of Austria snapped it up and set about modernising it. The Comte de Chambord (aka King Henry V of France in exile) continued the work, while the Franchetti family, who lived here after independence, restored its Gothic fairy-tale look and introduced a fantastical art nouveau staircase dripping with dragons. It's now used for art exhibitions, although the works have to compete with show-stopping Murano chandeliers. (Istituto Veneto di Scienze Lettere ed Arti; 041 240 77 11; www.palazzofranchetti.it; Campo Santo Stefano 2842; 10am-6pm Mon-Fri; Accademia)

Chiesa di Santa Maria del Giglio

CHURCH

8 Map p34, D5

Founded in the 9th century but almost completely rebuilt in the late 17th, this church is distinguished by a series of six relief maps on its facade featuring Rome and five cities which were Venetian possessions at the time: Padua, the Croatian cities of Zadar and Split, and the Greek cities of Heraklion and Corfu. Inside are some intriguing masterpieces. (Santa Maria Zobenigo; www.chorusvenezia.org; Campo di Santa Maria del Giglio; €3, with Chorus Pass free; 10.30am-4.30pm Mon-Sat; Giglio)

Scala Contarini del Bovolo

NOTABLE BUILDING

9 Map p34, E3

Under the republic, only the church and state were permitted to erect towers, as they could conceivably be used for military purposes. In around 1400 the Contarini family,

Understand

Keeping Venice Afloat

Impossible though it seems, Venetians built their home on 117 small islands connected by some 400 bridges over 150 canals. But if floating marble palaces boggle the mind, consider what's underneath them: an entire forest's worth of petrified wood pylons, rammed through silty *barene* (shoals) into the clay lagoon floor.

High Tides

Venice is ingeniously constructed to contend with lagoon tides, so even a four-alarm *acqua alta* (exceptionally high tide) is rarely cause for panic. But on 4 November 1966, record floods poured into 16,000 Venetian homes in terrifying waves, and residents were stranded in the wreckage of 1400 years of civilisation. Thanks to Venice's international appeal, assistance poured in and Unesco coordinated 50 private organisations to redress the ravages of the flood.

Cleaning up after *acqua alta* is a tedious job for Venetians: pumping water out of flooded ground floors and preventing corrosion by scrubbing salt residue off surfaces. Venice's canals must also be regularly dredged, which involves pumping water out, removing pungent sludge, then patching brickwork by hand with a ticklish technique Venetians call *scuci-cuci*.

Environmental Challenges

Venice and its lagoon are a Unesco World Heritage site – but in the wake of Tuscany's 2012 *Costa Concordia* shipwreck, Unesco expressed concern about the impact of cruise ships and unsustainable tourism. Italy's Port Authority has proposed rerouting cruise ships to Venice via inland Porta Marghera, bypassing Giudecca Canal. But critics like Venice's No Grandi Navi (No Big Ships) committee oppose cruise-ship entry into the lagoon due to pollution, including canalbank-corroding sulphur waste. Alternative seaward ports have been proposed at Malamocco.

Meanwhile, responsible travellers are taking action – eating sustainably sourced, local food; conserving water; using products free of industrial chemicals; and above all, supporting local businesses – to help offset tourism impact, and keep Venice afloat.

eager to show off their wealth and power, cheekily built this non-tower instead. Combining Venetian Gothic, Byzantine and Renaissance elements, this romantic 'staircase' looks even higher than its 26m due to the simple trick of decreasing the height of the arches as it rises. (041 309 66 05; www.scalacontarinidelbovolo.com; Calle Contarini del Bovolo 4299; adult/reduced €7/6; 10am-6pm; Sant'Angelo)

Negozio Olivetti ARCHITECTURE

10 Map p34, F4

Like a revolver pulled from a petticoat, ultramodern Negozio Olivetti was an outright provocation when it first appeared under the frilly arcades of the Procuratie Vecchie in 1958. High-tech pioneer Olivetti commissioned Venetian architect Carlo Scarpa to transform a narrow, dim souvenir shop into a showcase for its sleek typewriters and 'computing machines' (several 1948–54 models are displayed). (Olivetti Store; 041 522 83 87; www.negoziolivetti.it; Piazza San Marco 101; adult/reduced €6/3; 10.30am-5.30pm Tue-Sun; San Marco)

Eating

Ristorante Quadri MODERN ITALIAN €€€

11 Map p34, G3

When it comes to Venetian glamour, nothing beats this historic Michelin-starred restaurant overlooking Piazza San Marco. A small swarm of servers greets you as you're shown to your table in a room decked out with silk damask, gilt, painted beams and Murano chandeliers. Dishes are precise and delicious, deftly incorporating Venetian touches into an inventive modern Italian menu. (041 522 21 05; www.alajmo.it; Piazza San Marco 121; meals €110-138; 12.30-2.30pm & 7.30-10.30pm Tue-Sun; San Marco)

Bistrot de Venise VENETIAN €€€

12 Map p34, F3

Indulge in some culinary time travel at this fine-dining bistro where they've revived the recipes of Renaissance chef Bartolomeo Scappi. Dine like a doge in the red-and-gilt dining room on braised duck with wild apple and onion pudding, or enjoy the Jewish recipe of goose, raisin and pine-nut pasta. Even the desserts are beguilingly exotic. (041 523 66 51; www.bistrotdevenise.com; Calle dei Fabbri 4685; meals €47-78; noon-3pm & 7pm-midnight; ; Rialto)

Trattoria Da Fiore VENETIAN €€€

13 Map p34, C4

Rustic-chic decor sets the scene for excellent Venetian dishes composed of carefully selected seasonal ingredients from small Veneto producers. The restaurant is justly famous for its seafood dishes. Next door, the bar's *cicheti* (Venetian tapas) counter serves tasty snacks at more democratic prices. (041 523 53 10;

BUMBLE DEE/SHUTTERSTOCK ©

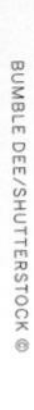

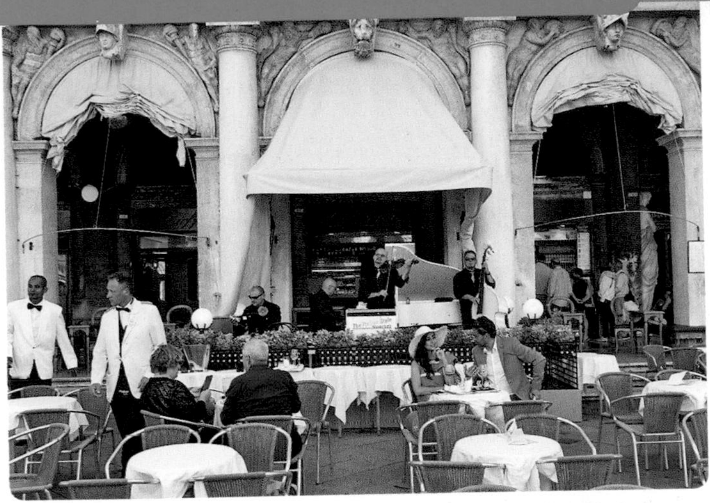

Caffè Florian (p33)

www.dafiore.it; Calle de le Botteghe 3461; meals €46-62; ⏲12.30-2.30pm & 7.30-10.30pm; ⛴San Samuele)

Ai Mercanti

ITALIAN €€

14 Map p34, E3

With its pumpkin-coloured walls, gleaming golden fixtures and jet-black tables and chairs, Ai Mercanti effortlessly conjures up a romantic mood. No wonder dates whisper over glasses of wine from the vast selection before tucking into modern bistro-style dishes. Although there's a focus on seafood and secondary cuts of meat, there are some wonderful vegetarian options as well. (☎041 523 82 69; www.aimercanti.it; Corte Coppo 4346a; meals €34-38; ⏲11.30am-3pm & 7-10pm Tue-Sat, 7-11pm Mon; ⛴Rialto)

Marchini Time

BAKERY €

15 Map p34, E2

Elbow your way through the morning crush to bag a warm croissant filled with runny apricot jam or melting Nutella. Everything here is freshly baked, which is why the crowd hangs around as croissants give way to foccacia, *pizette* (mini pizzas) and generously stuffed *panini*. (☎041 241 30 87; www.marchinitime.it; Campo San Luca 4589; items €1.20-3.50; ⏲7.30am-8.30pm; ⛴Rialto)

Suso
GELATO €

16 Map p34, F1

Indulge in gelato as rich as a doge, in original seasonal flavours like marscapone cream with fig sauce and walnuts. All Suso's gelati are locally made and free of artificial colours; gluten-free cones are available. (348 564 65 45; www.gelatovenezia.it; Calle de la Bissa 5453; scoops €1.60; 10am-midnight; Rialto)

Osteria da Carla
VENETIAN €€

17 Map p34, F4

Diners in the know duck into this hidden courtyard, less than 100m from Piazza San Marco, to snack on *cicheti* at the counter or to sit down to a romantic meal. The surroundings are at once modern and ancient, with exposed brick and interesting art. (041 523 78 55; www.osteriadacarla.it; Corte Contarina 1535a; meals €43-48; 8.30am-11pm Mon-Sat; San Marco)

Rosa Salva
BAKERY €

18 Map p34, F2

With just-baked strudel and reliable cappuccino, Rosa Salva has provided Venetians with fresh reasons to roll out of bed for over a century. Cheerfully efficient women working the spotless counter supply gale-force espresso and turbo-loaded pistachio profiteroles to power you across 30 more bridges. (041 522 79 34; www.rosasalva.it; Mercerie 5020; items €1.30-7.50; 8am-8pm; Rialto)

Rosticceria Gislon
VENETIAN, DELI €

19 Map p34, F1

Serving San Marco workers since the 1930s, this no-frills *rosticceria* (roast-meat specialist) has an ultramarine canteen counter downstairs and a small eat-in restaurant upstairs. Hot to trot you'll find *arancini* (rice balls), deep-fried mozzarella balls, croquettes and fish fry-ups. No one said it was going to be healthy! (041 522 35 69; Calle de la Bissa 5424; meals €15-25; 9am-9.30pm Tue-Sun, to 3.30pm Mon; Rialto)

Drinking

Grancaffè Quadri
CAFE

20 Map p34, G3

Powdered wigs seem appropriate inside this baroque bar-cafe, serving happy hours since 1638. During Carnevale, costumed Quadri revellers party like it's 1699 – despite prices shooting up to €15 a *spritz*. Grab a seat on the piazza to watch the best show in town: the sunset sparking the basilica's golden mosaics ablaze. (041 522 21 05; www.alajmo.it; Piazza San Marco 121; 9am-midnight; San Marco)

Bar Longhi
COCKTAIL BAR

21 Map p34, D5

The Gritti's beautiful Bar Longhi may be hellishly expensive, but if you consider the room – with its Fortuny fabrics, intarsia marble bar,

18th-century mirrors and million-dollar Piero Longhi paintings – its signature orange martini (the work of art that it is) starts to seem reasonable. In summer you'll have to choose between the twinkling interior and a spectacular Grand Canal terrace. (041 79 47 81; www.hotelgrittipalacevenice.com; Campo di Santa Maria del Giglio 2467; 11am-1am; Giglio)

Harry's Bar

BAR

22 Map p34, F5

Aspiring auteurs hold court at tables well scuffed by Ernest Hemingway, Charlie Chaplin, Truman Capote and Orson Welles, enjoying the signature €22 bellini (Giuseppe Cipriani's original 1948 recipe: white peach juice and *prosecco*) with a side of reflected glory. (041 528 57 77; www.harrysbarvenezia.com; Calle Vallaresso 1323; 10.30am-11pm; San Marco)

L'Ombra del Leoni

BAR

23  Map p34, F5

Lucky Biennale workers have Grand Canal views from their upstairs offices in Ca' Giustinian, but you too can enjoy the *palazzo's* peerless waterside position in the downstairs cafe-restaurant. Try to nab a seat on the outdoor terrace – it's the perfect spot to watch the gondolas come and go, with basilicas as the backdrop. (041 521 87 11; Calle Ridotto 1364a; 9am-midnight summer, to 9pm winter; San Marco)

Top Tip

Coffee or Rent?

In San Marco the price of a sit-down coffee seems more like rent. Take your coffee standing at a bar like the locals do for €1 to €2.50. If you want to luxuriate inside the baroque cafes in Piazza San Marco, or idle in the outdoor seating, there's usually a €6 surcharge. Still, you do get to enjoy a top-class classical orchestra and one of the best views in the world.

Teamo

WINE BAR

24  Map p34, D3

By day it's more of a cafe, but in the evening the little tables fill up with a mixed crowd, drinking wine and snacking on massive platters of *salumi* (cured meats) and cheese. (041 528 37 87; www.teamowinebar.com; Rio Terà de la Mandola 3795; 8.30am-10.30pm Fri-Wed; Sant'Angelo)

Enoteca al Volto

WINE BAR

25  Map p34, D2

Join the crowd working its way through the vast selection of *cicheti* in this historic wood-panelled bar that feels like the inside of a ship's hold. Lining the ceiling above the golden glow of the brass bar lanterns are hundreds of wine labels from just some of the bottles of regional wines that are cracked open every night. (041 522 89 45; Calle Cavalli 4081; 10am-3pm & 6-11pm; Rialto)

MARTIN NORRIS/ALAMY ©

Bellinis at Harry's Bar (p43)

Black-Jack

WINE BAR

26 Map p34, E2

Staff dispense delicious *cicheti* from a central horseshoe-shaped bar in this upmarket little place in the main shopping precinct. It's a great place for a snack and a tipple on your way to La Fenice or Teatro Goldoni; you could easily make a meal of it. (Campo San Luca 4267b; 7.30am-9pm; Rialto)

Entertainment

La Fenice

OPERA

27 Map p34, D4

One of Italy's top opera houses, La Fenice stages a rich roster of opera, ballet and classical music. The cheapest seats are in the boxes at the top, nearest the stage. The view is extremely restricted, but you will get to hear the music, watch the orchestra, soak up the atmosphere and people-watch. (041 78 66 72; www.teatrolafenice.it; Campo San Fantin 1977; restricted view from €30; Giglio)

Teatro Goldoni

THEATRE

28 Map p34, E2

Named after the city's great playwright, Venice's main theatre has an impressive dramatic range that runs from Goldoni's comedy to Shakespearean tragedy (mostly in Italian), plus ballets and concerts. Don't be fooled by the huge 20th-century bronze doors: this venerable theatre dates from 1622, and the jewel-box interior seats just 800. (041 240 20 14; www.teatrostabileveneto.it; Calle del Teatro 4650b; Rialto)

Shopping

Chiarastella Cattana

HOMEWARES

29 Map p34, B4

Transform any home into a thoroughly modern *palazzo* with these locally woven, strikingly original Venetian linens. Whimsical cushions feature chubby purple rhinoceroses and grumpy scarlet elephants straight out of Pietro Longhi paintings, and hand-tasselled jacquard hand towels will dry your royal guests in style. Decorators and design aficionados, save an afternoon to consider dizzying woven-to-order napkin and curtain options here. (041 522 43 69; www.chiarastellacattana.com; Salizada San Samuele 3216; 11am-1pm & 3-7pm Mon-Sat; San Samuele)

L'Armadio di Coco Luxury Vintage

VINTAGE

30 Map p34, D5

Jam-packed with pre-loved designer treasures from yesteryear, this tiny shop is the place to come when you're looking for classic Chanel dresses, exquisite cashmere coats and limited-edition Gucci shoulder bags. (041 241 32 14; www.larmadiodicoco.it; Campo di Santa Maria del Giglio 2516a; 10.30am-7.30pm; Giglio)

L'Isola

GLASS

31 Map p34, B4

Backlit chalices and spotlit vases emit an other-worldly glow at this shrine to Murano modernist glass master Carlo Moretti. Geometric shapes contain freeform swirls of orange and red, and glasses etched with fish-scale patterns add wit and a wink to high-minded modernism. Prices for signature water glasses start at €105. (041 523 19 73; www.lisola.com; Calle de la Botteghe 2970; 10.30am-7.30pm; San Samuele)

Understand

Wagner Says 'Shhhh!'

By the 19th century, Venice's great families were largely ruined and could not afford to heat their enormous *palazzi* (mansions). La Fenice served as a members-only club where Venetian society would spend much of the day gambling, gossiping and providing running commentary during performances. When he first performed at La Fenice, German composer Richard Wagner miffed the notoriously chatty Venetian opera crowd by insisting on total silence during performances.

Esperienze

GLASS, FASHION

32 Map p34, G2

When an Italian minimalist falls in love with a Murano glass-blower, the result is spare, spirited glass jewellery. Esperienze is a collaborative effort for husband-wife team Graziano and Sara: he breathes life into her designs, including matte-glass teardrop pendants and cracked-ice earrings. They also stock a range of women's clothing. (041 521 29 45; www.esperienzevenezia.com; Calle dei Specchieri 473b; 10am-noon & 3-7pm; San Marco)

Atelier Segalin di Daniela Ghezzo

SHOES

33 Map p34, E3

A gold chain pulled across this historic atelier doorway means Daniela is already consulting with a client, discussing rare leathers while taking foot measurements. Each pair is custom-made, so you'll never see your emerald ostrich-leather boots on another diva, or your dimpled manta-ray brogues on a rival mogul. Expect to pay around €1000 and wait six weeks for delivery. (041 522 21 15; www.danielaghezzo.it; Calle dei Fuseri 4365; 10am-1pm & 3-7pm Mon-Fri, 10am-1pm Sat; San Marco)

Venetia Studium

FASHION & ACCESSORIES

34 Map p34, D5

Get that 'just got in from Monaco for my art opening' look beloved of bohemians who marry well. The high-drama Delphos tunic dresses make anyone look like a high-maintenance modern dancer or heiress (Isadora Duncan and Peggy Guggenheim were both fans), and the hand-stamped silk-velvet bags are more arty than ostentatious. (041 523 69 53; www.venetiastudium.com; Calle de le Ostreghe 2427; 10am-7.30pm; Giglio)

Ottica Carraro

FASHION & ACCESSORIES

35 Map p34, D3

Lost your sunglasses on the Lido? Never fear: Ottica Carraro can make you a custom pair within 24 hours, including the eye exam. The store has its own limited-edition 'Venice' line, ranging from cat-eye shades perfect for facing paparazzi to chunky wood-grain frames that could get you mistaken for an art critic at the Biennale. (041 520 42 58; www.otticacarraro.it; Calle de la Mandola 3706; 9.30am-1pm & 3-7.30pm Mon-Sat; Sant'Angelo)

Camuffo

GLASS

36 Map p34, F2

Kids, entomologists and glass collectors seek out Signor Camuffo in this cabinet of miniature natural wonders. Expect to find him wielding a blowtorch as he fuses metallic foils and molten glass into shimmering wings for the city's finest worked glass beetles and dragonflies. Between bugs, he'll chat about his

ALEX ARMITAGE/ALAMY ©

Fortuny silk lamps at Venetia Studium

work and sell you strands of Murano glass beads. (Calle de le Acque 4992; 10am-5pm Mon-Sat; Rialto)

Venetian Dreams

FASHION & ACCESSORIES

37 Map p34, D3

High fashion meets *acqua alta* in Marisa Convento's aquatic accessories. La Fenice divas demand her freshwater-pearl-encrusted velvet handbags, while Biennale artistes snap up octopus-tentacle glass-bead necklaces. Between customers, Marisa can be glimpsed at her desk, painstakingly weaving coral-branch collars from antique Murano *conterie* (seed beads). To wow Carnevale crowds, ask about custom costume orders. (041 523 02 92; www.venetiandreams.altervista.org; Calle de la Mandola 3805a; 11am-6.30pm Wed-Mon; Sant'Angelo)

Explore

Dorsoduro & the Accademia

Dorsoduro covers prime Grand Canal waterfront with Ca' Rezzonico's gilded splendour, the Peggy Guggenheim Collection's modern edge, Gallerie dell'Accademia's Renaissance beauties and Punta della Dogana's ambitious installation art. The neighbourhood lazes days away on the sun-drenched Zattere, and convenes in Campo Santa Margherita for *spritz* (*prosecco* cocktails) and flirtation.

The Sights in a Day

Brace yourself with a cappuccino at **Il Caffè Rosso** (p55) for an epic journey through eight centuries of Venetian masterpieces at **Gallerie dell'Accademia** (p50). Afterwards, recover your senses over canalside *panini* (sandwiches) at **Cantinone Già Schiavi** (p63).

Revived, see how Pollock splatter-paintings and Calder mobiles make a splash along the Grand Canal at the **Peggy Guggenheim Collection** (p52), then argue the merits of Jeff Koons, Damien Hirst and other controversial installation artists at **Punta della Dogana** (p58). Pop next door and let the mysterious powers of the **Basilica di Santa Maria della Salute** (pictured left, background; p58) restore your peace of mind, before it's boggled by Vedova's robotic art displays at **Fondazione Vedova** (p60) or Veronese's floor-to-ceiling masterpieces at **Chiesa di San Sebastiano** (p58).

Enjoy stunning fuschia sunsets on the Giudecca Canal with a *spritz* at **El Chioschetto** (p63) before dining on lagoon seafood at **Riviera** (p60). Just don't be late for the baroque concerto at **Scuola Grande dei Carmini** (p59) or the latest bossa nova beats at **Venice Jazz Club** (p64).

For a local's day in Dorsoduro, see p54.

Top Sights

Local Life

Best of Venice

Museums

Eating

Getting There

Vaporetto Grand Canal 1, 2 and N lines stop at Accademia; line 1 also calls at Ca' Rezzonico and Salute. Lines 5.1, 5.2, 6 and the N (night) stop at the Zattere and/or San Basilio. Airport lines stop at Zattere.

Top Sights
Gallerie dell'Accademia

Hardly academic, these galleries contain more murderous intrigue, forbidden romance and shameless politicking than the most outrageous Venetian parties. The former Santa Maria della Carità convent complex maintained its serene composure for centuries, but ever since Napoleon installed his haul of Venetian art trophies in 1807, there's been nonstop visual drama inside these walls.

Map p56, E4

041 520 03 45

www.gallerieaccademia.org

Campo della Carità 1050

adult/reduced €12/6

8.15am-2pm Mon, to 7.15pm Tue-Sun

Accademia

Feast in the House of Levi, Paolo Veronese

Carpaccio
UFO arrivals seem imminent in the glowing skies of Carpaccio's gruesome *Crucifixion* and *Glorification of the Ten Thousand Martyrs of Mount Ararat* (Room 2).

Tintoretto
The Venetian Renaissance master's *Creation of the Animals* (Room 6) is a fantastical bestiary suggesting God put forth his best efforts inventing Venetian seafood (no argument here).

Titian
His 1576 *Pietà* (Room 6) was possibly finished posthumously by Palma il Giovane, but notice the smears of paint Titian applied with his bare hands and the column-base self-portrait.

Veronese
Paolo Veronese's restored *Feast in the House of Levi* (Room 10) was originally called *Last Supper*, until Inquisition leaders condemned it for showing dogs and drunkards, among others, cavorting with Apostles. Veronese refused to change a thing besides the title.

Portrait Galleries
Lock eyes with Lorenzo Lotto's soul-searching *Portrait of a Young Scholar*, Rosalba Carriera's brutally honest self-portrait and Pietro Longhi's lovestruck violinist in *The Dance Lesson*.

Sala dell'Albergo
The Accademia's grand finale is the Sala dell'Albergo, with a lavishly carved ceiling, Antonio Vivarini's wraparound 1441–50 masterpiece of fluffy-bearded saints, and Titian's 1534–39 *Presentation of the Virgin*.

☑ Top Tips

- Free admission the first Sunday of month.
- To skip ahead of the queues in high season, book tickets in advance online (booking fee €1.50).
- Queues are shorter in the afternoon; last entry is 45 minutes before closing, but a proper visit takes at least 1½ hours.
- The audio guide (€6) is mostly descriptive and largely unnecessary – avoid the wait and follow your bliss and the explanatory wall tags.
- Bags larger than 20x30x15cm need to be stored in the lockers, which require a refundable €1 coin.

Take a Break

Starving artists and gallery-goers descend on Bar alla Toletta (p62) for grilled-to-order *panini*.

Top Sights
Peggy Guggenheim Collection

After tragically losing her father on the *Titanic,* heiress Peggy Guggenheim befriended Dadaists, dodged Nazis and changed art history at her palatial home on the Grand Canal. Peggy's Palazzo Venier dei Leoni is a showcase for surrealism, futurism and abstract expressionism by some 200 breakthrough modern artists, including Peggy's ex-husband Max Ernst and Jackson Pollock (among her many rumoured lovers).

Map p56, F4

041 240 54 11

www.guggenheim-venice.it

Palazzo Venier dei Leoni 704

adult/reduced €15/9

10am-6pm Wed-Mon

Accademia

Modernist Collection

Peggy Guggenheim escaped Paris two days before the Nazi invasion, and boldly defied established social and artistic dictates. She collected according to her own convictions, featuring folk art and lesser-known artists alongside such radical early modernists as Kandinsky, Picasso, Man Ray, Rothko, Mondrian, Joseph Cornell and Dalí.

Italian Avant-Garde

Upon her 1948 arrival in Venice, Peggy became a spirited advocate for contemporary Italian art, which had largely gone out of favour with the rise of Mussolini and the partisan politics of WWII. Her support led to reappraisals of Umberto Boccioni, Giorgio Morandi, Giacomo Balla, Giuseppe Capogrossi and Giorgio de Chirico, and aided Venice's own Emilio Vedova and Giuseppe Santomaso. Never afraid to make a splash, Peggy gave passing gondoliers an eyeful on her Grand Canal quay: Marino Marini's 1948 *Angel of the City,* a bronze male nude on horseback visibly excited by the possibilities on the horizon.

Sculpture Garden

Peggy's palace was never finished, but that didn't stop her from filling every space indoors and out with art. In the sculpture garden, wander past bronzes by Henry Moore, Alberto Giacometti and Constantin Brancusci, Yoko Ono's *Wish Tree* and a shiny black-granite lump by Anish Kapoor. The city of Venice granted an honorary dispensation for Peggy to be buried beneath the Giacometti sculptures, alongside her dearly departed lapdogs.

☑ Top Tips

- Excellent audio guides (€7) are available in Italian, English, German, French and Spanish.
- Free daily presentations in Italian and English are given on the life of Peggy Guggenheim (noon and 4pm) and individual works in the collection (11am and 5pm).
- If you spot someone wearing an 'Ask me about the Art' badge feel free to quiz them. They are Guggenheim interns in training.
- In May and June the gallery hosts Happy Spritz evenings featuring live music in the sculpture garden.

Take a Break

The gallery's pavilion cafe offers respectable espresso, light lunches and high tea with views over the sculpture garden.

Local Life
Happy Hour in Campo Santa Margherita

By day Campo Santa Margherita hosts a weekday fish market, the odd flea market and periodic political protests, but by six o'clock this unruly square becomes Venice's nightlife hub. Just don't try to pack it all into one happy hour. Pace yourself on your *giro d'ombra* (pub crawl), lest you end up in the drink of a nearby canal.

❶ Snacks at Bakarò

'Permesso!' (Pardon!) is the chorus inside this historic **bar** (Calle della Chiesa 3665; ⏲10am-1am; ⛴Ca' Rezzonico), where the crowd spills onto the sidewalk and tries not to spill drinks in the process. Arrive at the tiny wooden bar early for the best choice of 45-plus wines by the glass and respectable *tramezzini* (sandwiches).

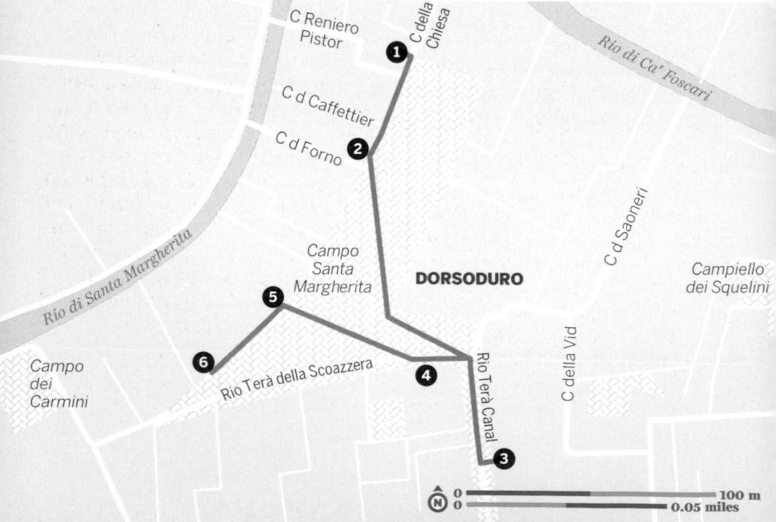

❷ Spritz at Il Caffè Rosso

Locals affectionately call this red **storefront** (041 528 79 98; www.cafferosso.it; Campo Santa Margherita 2963; 7am-1am Mon-Sat; ; Ca' Rezzonico) '*al rosso*' (the red), and its inexpensive *spritz* (*prosecco* cocktail) generously splashed with scarlet Aperol gives visitors and locals alike an instant flush of Venetian colour. Plan to arrive when the clock strikes '*spritz* o'clock' at 6pm sharp, and mingle with standing-room-only crowds.

❸ Cocktails at Imagina Café

For your next stop, branch out to top-shelf cocktails served at this sleek, backlit **bar** (041 241 06 25; www.imaginacafe.it; Rio Terà Canal 3126; 7am-9pm Sun-Thu, to 1am Fri & Sat; ; Ca' Rezzonico) surrounded by local art. The creative, chatty and gay-friendly crowd here should probably start paying rent at outdoor tables, while their sweater-clad dogs bask in the admiration of passers-by.

❹ Ice Cream Fit for a Doge at Gelateria Il Doge

If you're wondering what the crowd is at the southern end of the *campo* (square), it's the mob eyeing up the impossibly good selection of gelato at this venerable **ice-cream parlour** (389 1288965; www.gelateriaildoge.com; Campo Santa Margherita 3058a; scoops from €1.50; 8am-midnight summer, to 11pm winter; ; Ca' Rezzonico). Have a bar break and join the gang shouting out orders for pink Himalayan salt, fig and caramel swirl and refreshing Sicilian lemon *granita* (sorbet).

❺ Flirting at Osteria alla Bifora

While *spritz*-pounding students carouse outside in the *campo*, gentle flirting ensues in this chandelier-lit medieval **wine cave** (041 523 61 19; Campo Santa Margherita 2930; noon-3pm & 5pm-2am Wed-Mon; Ca' Rezzonico) over big-hearted Veneto merlot. While you wait for a platter of cheese and carved-to-order cured meats to arrive, you'll make newfound friends at communal tables.

❻ Late-Night Munchies at Orient Experience II

Despite its dialogue with the East, Venice lacks good ethnic eateries, but this wildly popular **Eastern deli** (041 520 02 17; Campo Santa Margherita 2920; meals €12-18; 11.30am-11pm; Ca' Rezzonico) aims to set that straight. Run by Ahmed, it dishes up colourful bowls of Afghan, Iranian, Turkish and Maghrebi cuisine to hungry students, curious Venetians and adventurous travellers. Round it all off with a delicious cup of cardamom coffee and some pistachio baklava.

A
B
C
D
1
2
3
4
5
Rio dei Tre Ponti
Fond del Rio Novo
C e Corte Basego
Campiello Mosca
C d Preti Crosera
C del Scaleter
Fond d Forner
C del Campaniel
C San Pantalon
Campo S Pantalon
C Crosera
C della Saoneria
C Larga Foscari
C Marcona
C Larga Ragusei
Corte Contarini
C della Chiesa
C Reniero Pistor
Rio di Ca' Foscari
Fond Rossa
Rio Briati
C Ragusei
Rio di Santa Margherita
C d Forno
C d Magazen
C dell' Aseo
C d Saoneri
Campiello dei Squelini
Grand Canal
Campo Santa Margherita
Fond Foscarini
Scuola Grande dei Carmini
C del Cappeller
Fond Briati
Fond del Soccorso
Rio dei Carmini
Rio Terà della Scoazzera
C delle Pazienze
Rio Terà Canal
C Bernardo
San Samuele
C delle Botteghe
Ca' Rezzonico
Rio Terà Scoazzera
Fond Alberti
Fond Rezzonico
Campo S Samuele
Fond di San Sebastiano
Fond de la Squero
Fond Gheradini
Campo San Barnaba
C del Traghetto
Ca' Rezzonico
Rio di San Barnaba
Corte Zappa
C del Lombardo
Rio di San Sebastian
C Lunga San Barnaba
C del Cerchieri
Rio dell'Avogaria
C de l'Avogaria
C d Degolin
C dei Puti
Rio Malpaga
Fond della Toletta
Rio della Toletta
Chiesa di San Sebastiano
C Balastro
Fond San Basegio
Rio Terà Ognissanti
Fond de la Romite
Fond di Borgo
C d Eremite
C Forno
C d Toletta
Fond Bonlini
C Corfù
C della Chiesa
Campo San Basegio
C dei Preti
C della Masena
Fond Ognissanti
C dei Frati
Rio Terà Carità
Old Stazione Marittima
C dei Cartelotti
Corte Canal
Rio di Ognissanti
DORSODURO
Fond Priuli
C del Pistor
San Basilio
Fond Bonlini
Campo S Trovaso
C Larga Nani
C Trevisan
Fond Zattere al Ponte Lungo
C Larga Pisani
Fond Nani
Ponte Lungo
C dei Frati
Zattere Ponte Lungo
Canale di Fusina
Fond delle Zattere
Rio Terà Antonio Foscarini
Alilaguna
1
2
3
4
5
8
9
10
11
12
13
14
15
16
17
18
19
20
21
22
23
24
26
29
30
31
32

E
F
G
H
1
2
3
4
5
0 200 m
0 0.1 miles
For reviews see
Top Sights p50
Sights p58
Eating p60
Drinking p63
Entertainment p64
Shopping p65
Sant'Angelo
San Tomà
Rio di Ca'Santi
Corte de l'Albero
Rio di Sant'Angelo
C dei Avvocati
C Pesaro
C de la Mandola
C Mocenigo Ca' Vecchia
Ramo Lezze
Saliz S Samuele
Piscina S Samuele
C del Pestrin
C d Caffettier
C de la Verona
Rio de la Verona
Rio dei Barcaroli
Frezzaria
Piscina Frezzaria
C del Carro
Campo S Anzolo
C dei Frati
C de le Botteghe
C de le Carrozze
Saliz Malipiero
C d Muneghe
C dei Orbi
C Caotorta
C della Fenice
Ramo Primo dei Calegheri
SAN MARCO
Rio de la Veste
C Veste
Campo di San Moisè
Campo Santo Stefano
C Spezier
Rio Malatin
Fond della Malvasia Vecchia
Campo S Maurizio
C Larga XXII Marzo
Rio del Duca
C Vitturi
C Giustinian
Campo di S Vidal
C del Dose da Ponte
Fond Corner Zaguri
Rio di San Maurizio
C de le Ostreghe
Campo di Santa Maria del Giglio
C Pedrocchi
C del Traghetto
C Squero
Corte Barozzi
Ponte dell'Accademia
Rio dell'Orso
C Gritti
Campo Traghetto
Santa Maria del Giglio Traghetto
Campo della Carità
Gallerie dell'Accademia
Peggy Guggenheim Collection
Fond Dogana alla Salute
Salute
Punta della Dogana
Palazzo Cini
Campo San Vio
Piscina Forner
6
C Pompea
C d Chiesa
25
C S Cristoforo
C d Bastion
Campo della Salute
2
Fond Venier dei Leoni
28
C dell'Abbazia
1
Basilica di Santa Maria della Salute
Piscina Venier
Fond de Ca' Bragadin
C Franchi
Fond Ospedaleto
27
Fond della Salute
Fond Venier
Rio Terà Catecumeni
Piscina S Agnese
C Capuzzi
Corte Nuova
C Molin
Fond Soranzo della Fornace
C dello Squero
Rio della Salute
Fond Zattere al Saloni
C d Squero
C Navaro
Rio Terà di San Vio
Fond di Ca' Balà
C da Ponte
Rio di San Vio
C degli Incurabili
Rio delle Torselle
Fondazione Vedova
7
Fond Zattere Santo Spirito
Rio delle Fornace

Sights

Basilica di Santa Maria della Salute BASILICA

1 Map p56, H4

Guarding the entrance to the Grand Canal, this 17th-century domed church was commissioned by Venice's plague survivors as thanks for their salvation. Baldassare Longhena's uplifting design is an engineering feat that defies simple logic; in fact, the church is said to have mystical curative properties. Titian eluded the plague until age 94, leaving 12 key paintings in the basilica's art-slung sacristy. (La Salute; www.basilicasalutevenezia.it; Campo della Salute 1b; basilica free, sacristy adult/reduced €4/2; basilica 9.30am-noon & 3-5.30pm, sacristry 10am-noon & 3-5pm Mon-Sat, 3-5pm Sun; Salute)

Punta della Dogana GALLERY

2 Map p56, H4

Fortuna, the weather vane atop Punta della Dogana, swung Venice's way in 2005, when bureaucratic hassles in Paris convinced art collector François Pinault to showcase his works in Venice's long-abandoned customs warehouses. Built by Giuseppe Benoni in 1677 to ensure no ship entered the Grand Canal without paying duties, the warehouses reopened in 2009 after a striking reinvention by Tadao Ando. The dramatic space now hosts exhibitions of ambitious, large-scale contemporary artworks from some of the world's most provocative creative minds. (041 271 90 39; www.palazzograssi.it; Fondamente della Dogana alla Salute 2; adult/reduced €15/10, incl Palazzo Grassi €18/15; 10am-7pm Wed-Mon Apr-Nov; Salute)

Ca' Rezzonico MUSEUM

3 Map p56, D2

Baroque dreams come true at Baldassare Longhena's Grand Canal palace, where a marble staircase leads to gilded ballrooms, frescoed salons and sumptuous boudoirs. Giambattista Tiepolo's Throne Room ceiling is a masterpiece of elegant social climbing, showing gorgeous Merit ascending to the Temple of Glory clutching the Golden Book of Venetian nobles' names – including Tiepolo's patrons, the Rezzonico family. (Museum of the 18th Century; 041 241 01 00; www.visitmuve.it; Fondamenta Rezzonico 3136; adult/reduced €10/7.50; 10am-6pm Wed-Mon summer, to 5pm winter; Ca' Rezzonico)

Chiesa di San Sebastiano CHURCH

4 Map p56, A3

Antonio Scarpignano's relatively austere 1508–48 facade creates a sense of false modesty at this neighbourhood church. Currently undergoing restoration, the interior is adorned with floor-to-ceiling masterpieces by Paolo Veronese, executed over three decades. According to popular local

Giambattista Tiepolo fresco in the Throne Room of Ca' Rezzonico

legend, Veronese found sanctuary at San Sebastiano in 1555 after fleeing murder charges in Verona, and his works in this church deliver lavish thanks to the parish and an especially brilliant poke in the eye of his accusers. (www.chorusvenezia.org; Campo San Sebastiano 1687; €3, with Chorus Pass free; 10.30am-4.30pm Mon-Sat; San Basilio)

Scuola Grande dei Carmini HISTORIC BUILDING

5 Map p56, B2

Eighteenth-century backpackers must have thought they'd died and gone to heaven at Scuola Grande dei Carmini, with its lavish interiors by Giambattista Tiepolo and Baldassare Longhena. The gold-leafed, Longhena-designed stucco stairway heads up towards Tiepolo's nine-panel ceiling of a rosy *Virgin in Glory*. The adjoining hostel room is bedecked in *boiserie* (wood carving). (041 528 94 20; www.scuolagrandecarmini.it; Campo Santa Margherita 2617; adult/reduced €5/4; 11am-5pm; Ca' Rezzonico)

Palazzo Cini GALLERY

6 Map p56, E4

This elegant 16th-century Gothic *palazzo* (mansion) was the former home of industrialist and philanthropist Vittorio Cini, who filled it with first-class Renaissance paintings, period furnishings, ceramics and Murano glass. Wonderful paintings by lesser known Renaissance lights such as Filippo Lippi, Piero di Cosimo and Dosso Dossi festoon the walls, their glowing brilliance even more impactful in these intimate, domestic spaces. (041 220 12 15; www.palazzocini.it; Campo San Vio 864; adult/reduced €10/8; 11am-7pm Wed-Mon mid-Apr–mid-Nov; Accademia)

Fondazione Vedova

GALLERY

7 Map p56, G5

A retrofit designed by Pritzker Prize–winning architect Renzo Piano transformed Venice's historic salt warehouses into Fondazione Vedova art galleries, commemorating pioneering Venetian abstract painter Emilio Vedova. Shows here are often literally moving and rotating: powered by renewable energy sources, 10 robotic arms designed by Vedova and Piano move major modern artworks in and out of storage slots. (Magazzini del Sale; 041 522 66 26; www.fondazionevedova.org; Fondamenta delle Zattere 266; adult/reduced €8/6; exhibitions 10.30am-6pm Wed-Mon; Zattere)

Top Tip

Sacred Music at Salute

If you think the Longhena-designed dome of the Basilica di Santa Maria della Salute (p58) looks magnificent, wait until you hear how it sounds. Weekdays at 3.30pm, vespers are played on the basilica's original 1782–83 organ. These musical interludes are free, and the acoustics are nothing short of celestial.

Eating

Riviera

VENETIAN €€€

8 Map p56, B4

Seafood connoisseurs concur that dining at GP Cremonini's restaurant is a Venetian highlight. A former rock musician, GP now focuses his considerable talents on delivering perfectly balanced octopus stew, feather-light gnocchi with lagoon crab, and risotto with langoustine and hop shoots. The setting, overlooking the Giudecca Canal, is similarly spectacular, encompassing views of Venetian domes backed by hot-pink sunsets. (041 522 76 21; www.ristoranteriviera.it; Fondamenta Zattere al Ponte Lungo 1473; meals €70-85; 12.30-3pm & 7-10.30pm Fri-Tue; Zattere)

Estro

VENETIAN, WINE BAR €€

9 Map p56, C1

Estro is anything you want it to be: wine bar, *aperitivo* pit stop, or sit-down degustation restaurant. The 500 wines – all of them naturally processed – are chosen by young-gun owners Alberto and Dario, whose passion for quality extends to the grub, from *cicheti* (Venetian tapas) topped with house-made *porchetta* (roast pork) to roasted guinea fowl and a succulent burger dripping with Asiago cheese. (☎041 476 49 14; www.estrovenezia.com; Calle dei Preti 3778; meals €35; ⊙11am-midnight Wed-Mon; ❄; ⛴San Tomà)

Enoteca Ai Artisti ITALIAN €€€

10 Map p56, C3

Indulgent cheeses, exceptional *nero di seppia* (cuttlefish ink) pasta, and tender *tagliata* (sliced steak) drizzled with aged balsamic vinegar atop rocket are paired with exceptional wines by the glass by your gracious oenophile hosts. Sidewalk tables for two make great people-watching, but book ahead for indoor tables for groups; space is limited. Note: only turf (no surf) dishes on Monday. (☎041 523 89 44; www.enotecaartisti.com; Fondamenta della Toletta 1169a; meals €45; ⊙noon-3pm & 7-10pm Mon-Sat; ⛴Ca' Rezzonico)

Pasticceria Tonolo PASTRIES €

11 Map p56, C1

Long, skinny Tonolo is the stuff of local legend, a fact confirmed by the never-ending queue of customers. Ditch packaged B&B croissants for flaky *apfelstrudel* (apple pastry), velvety *bignè al zabaione* (marsala cream pastry) and oozing *pain au chocolat* (chocolate croissants). Devour one at the bar with a bracing espresso, then bag another for the road. (☎041 532 72 09; Calle dei Preti 3764; pastries €1-4; ⊙7.45am-8pm Tue-Sat, 8am-1pm Sun, closed Sun Jul; ⛴Ca' Rezzonico)

Osteria Ai Do Farai VENETIAN €€

12 Map p56, C2

Venetian regulars pack this wood-panelled room, hung with nautical photographs and illustrations. The house mixed antipasto is a succulent prologue to dishes like pasta with shellfish and sweet prawns; herb-laced, grilled *orata* (bream); and Venetian *bis di saor sarde, scampi e sogliole* (sardines and prawns in tangy Venetian *saor* marinade). Service is leisurely; bide your time with a Negroni *aperitivo*. (☎041 277 03 69; Calle del Cappeller 3278; meals €25-35; ⊙noon-2.30pm & 7-10.30pm Mon-Sat; ⛴Ca' Rezzonico)

Da Codroma VENETIAN €€

13 Map p56, A2

In a city plagued by high prices and indifferent eating experiences, da Codroma wears its Slow Food badge of approval with pride. Chef Nicola faithfully maintains Venetian traditions here, serving up boiled baby octopi with a spritz of lemon and buckwheat *bigoli* pasta with anchovy sauce. It's a local favourite thanks to the quiet location and democratic prices. (☎041 524 67 89; www.osteriadacodroma.it; Fondamenta Briati 2540; meals €30-35; ⊙10am-4pm & 6-11.30pm Tue-Sat; ⛴San Basilio)

Cantinone Già Schiavi

Ristorante La Bitta

RISTORANTE €€

14 Map p56, C3

Recalling a cosy, woody bistro, La Bitta keeps punters purring with hearty rustic fare made using the freshest ingredients – no fish, just meat and seasonal veggies. Scan the daily menu for mouthwatering options like tagliatelle with artichoke thistle and gorgonzola or juicy pork *salsiccette* (small sausages) served with *verze* (local cabbage) and warming polenta. Reservations essential. Cash only. (041 523 05 31; Calle Lunga San Barnaba 2753a; meals €35-40; 6.30-11pm Mon-Sat; Ca' Rezzonico)

Bar alla Toletta

SANDWICHES €

15 Map p56, D3

Midway through museum crawls from Accademia to Ca' Rezzonico, Bar Toletta satisfies starving artists with lip-smacking, grilled-to-order *panini* (sandwiches), including *prosciutto crudo* (cured ham), rocket and mozzarella, and daily vegetarian options. *Tramezzini* (triangular stacked sandwiches) are tasty too – Bar Toletta goes easy on mayonnaise in favour of more flavourful toppings like olive tapenade. Get yours to go, or grab a seat for around €1 more. (041 520 01 96; Calle la Toletta 1192; sandwiches €1.60-5; 7am-8pm; ; Ca' Rezzonico)

Ai Quattro Feri

VENETIAN €€

16 Map p56, C3

Adorned with artworks by some well-known creative fans, this honest, good-humoured *osteria* (casual tavern) is well known for its simple, classic seafood dishes like al dente *spaghetti con seppie* (with cuttlefish), grilled *orata* (sea bream) and tender calamari. Post-meal coffees are made using a traditional Italian percolator for that homely, old-school feeling. No credit cards. (041 520 69 78; Calle Lunga San Barnaba 2754a; meals €35; 12.30-2.30pm & 7-10.30pm Mon-Sat; Ca' Rezzonico)

Drinking

Cantinone Già Schiavi

BAR

17 Map p56, D4

Regulars gamely pass along orders to timid newcomers, who might otherwise miss out on smoked swordfish *cicheti* with top-notch house Soave, or *pallottoline* (mini-bottles of beer) with generous *sopressa* (soft salami) *panini*. Chaos cheerfully prevails at this legendary canalside spot, where Accademia art historians rub shoulders with San Trovaso gondola builders without spilling a drop. (041 523 95 77; www.cantinaschiavi.com; Fondamenta Nani 992; 8.30am-8.30pm Mon-Sat; Zattere)

El Sbarlefo

BAR

18 Map p56, C1

If you're looking to escape the raucous student scene on Campo Santa Margherita, head to this grown-up bar with its chic industrial look, sophisticated rock and blues soundtrack, and live music at weekends. Aside from the long list of regional wines, there's a serious selection of spirits here. Accompany with plates of high-brow *cicheti* such as swordfish wrapped in robiola cheese. (041 524 66 50; www.elsbarlefo.it; Calle San Pantalon 3757; 10am-midnight; San Tomà)

El Chioschetto

BAR

19 Map p56, B4

There's really no better place to park yourself for *aperitivo* than at this pint-sized kiosk on the Zattere

Local Life

Squero di San Trovaso

The **wood-brick cabin** (Campo San Trovaso 1097, Dorsoduro; Zattere) along Rio di San Trovaso may look like a stray ski chalet, but it's one of Venice's handful of working *squeri* (shipyards), complete with refinished gondolas drying in the yard. When the door's open, you can peek inside in exchange for a donation left in the basket by the door. To avoid startling gondola-builders working with sharp tools, no flash photography is allowed.

overlooking the Giudecca Canal. Even on frosty spring evenings the tables fill up with a mixed crowd downing cocktails and *spritzes* and watching the spectacular Venetian sunset. In summer, on Wednesday and Saturday evenings, there's even live music. (☎348 3968466; Fondamente della Zattere al Ponte Lungo 1406a; ⏰8.30am-2am Mar-Nov; ⛴Zattere)

Caffè Bar Ai Artisti

BAR

20 Map p56, C3

The cast of characters who sweep into this tiny cafe throughout the day seem borrowed from Pietro Longhi's paintings at neighbouring Ca' Rezzonico. Bartenders aren't the least bit fazed by dashing caped strangers swilling double espresso, spaniels tucked underarm jealously eying the pastries, and Ca' Macana shoppers requesting straws to sip DOC *prosecco* through long-nosed plague doctor masks. (☎393 9680135; Campo San Barnaba 2771; ⏰7am-midnight Mon-Fri, 8am-midnight Sat, 9am-midnight Sun; ⛴Ca' Rezzonico)

Traghetto

Hop across the Grand Canal with the locals on the San Marco *traghetto* (passenger gondola), which connects Santa Maria del Giglio, 500m west of Piazza San Marco, to the Basilica di Santa Maria della Salute (San Gregorio stop), saving you a 40-minute walk. It costs €2 each way.

Ai Pugni

BAR

21  Map p56, C3

Centuries ago, brawls on the bridge out the front inevitably ended in the canal, but now Venetians settle differences with one of over 50 wines by the glass at this ever-packed bar, pimped with recycled Magnum-bottle lamps and wine-crate tables. The latest drops are listed on the blackboard, with *aperitivo*-friendly nibbles including *polpette* (meatballs) and cured local meats on bread. (☎041 523 98 31; Ponte dei Pugni 2859; ⏰8.30am-1am Mon-Sat, 10.30am-1am Sun; ⛴Ca' Rezzonico)

Entertainment

Venice Jazz Club

LIVE MUSIC

22  Map p56, C2

Jazz is alive and swinging in Dorsoduro, where the resident Venice Jazz Club Quartet pays regular respects to Miles Davis and John Coltrane, as well as heating up with Latin and bossa nova beats on Tuesday and Friday. Arrive by 8pm to pounce on complimentary cold-cut platters. The venue closes for all of August and much of January. (☎041 523 20 56; www.venicejazzclub.com; Ponte dei Pugni 3102; admission incl 1st drink €20; ⏰doors 7pm, set begins 9pm, closed Thu & Sun; ⛴Ca' Rezzonico)

Shopping

Ca' Macana

ARTS & CRAFTS

23 Map p56, C2

Glimpse the talents behind the Venetian Carnevale masks that impressed Stanley Kubrick so much he ordered several for his final film *Eyes Wide Shut*. Choose your papier-mâché persona from the selection of coquettish courtesan's eye-shades, chequered Casanova disguises and long-nosed plague doctor masks – or invent your own at Ca' Macana's mask-making workshops (one-hour per person €49, two-hour per person from €80). (041 277 61 42; www.camacana.com; Calle de le Botteghe 3172; 10am-7.30pm Sun-Fri, to 8pm Sat; Ca' Rezzonico)

Paolo Olbi

ARTS & CRAFTS

24 Map p56, C2

Thoughts worth committing to paper deserve Paolo Olbi's keepsake books, albums and stationery, whose fans include Hollywood actors and NYC mayors (ask to see the guestbook). Ordinary journals can't compare to Olbi originals, handmade with heavyweight paper and bound with exquisite leather bindings. The €1 watercolour postcards of Venice make for beautiful, bargain souvenirs. (041 523 76 55; http://olbi.atspace.com; Calle Foscari 3253a; 10.30am-12.40pm & 3.30-7.30pm Mon-Sat, 11.30am-12.40pm & 4-7.30pm Sun; Ca' Rezzonico)

Local Life

Soirées at the Scuola

Music and dancing in a religious institution? Rome tried to forbid it for centuries, but the Venetian tradition continues today at Scuola Grande dei Carmini with **Musica in Maschera** (Musical Masquerade; 041 528 76 67; www.musicainmaschera.it; Campo Santa Margherita 2617, Scuola Grande dei Carmini; tickets €22-85; 9pm Mar-Dec; Accademia), concerts performed in 1700s costume with opera singers and a ballet corps. Tickets are available downstairs at the Scuola (p59).

Marina e Susanna Sent

GLASS

25 Map p56, E4

Wearable waterfalls and soap-bubble necklaces are Venice style signatures, thanks to the Murano-born Sent sisters. Defying centuries-old beliefs that women can't handle molten glass, their minimalist statement jewellery is featured in museum stores worldwide, from Palazzo Grassi to MoMA. See new collections at this store, their flagship Murano studio, or the San Marco branch. (041 520 81 36; www.marinaesusannasent.com; Campo San Vio 669; 10am-1pm & 1.30-6.30pm; Accademia)

Madera

ACCESSORIES, HOMEWARES

26 Map p56, C3

Restyle your life at this modern design showcase, which stocks a sharply curated selection of Italian and international jewellery, accessories, homewares and gifts. The emphasis is on handmade and harder-to-find objects, whether it's sculptural chopping blocks and necklaces, or geometric serving trays and bags. (☎041 522 41 81; www.shopmaderavenezia.it; Campo San Barnaba 2762; ⏰10am-1pm & 3.30-7.30pm Tue-Sat; ⛴Ca' Rezzonico)

Antiquariato Claudia Canestrelli

ANTIQUES

27 Map p56, G4

Hand-coloured lithographs of fanciful lagoon fish, 19th-century miniatures of cats dressed as generals, and vintage cufflinks make for charming souvenirs of Venice's past in this walk-in curio cabinet. Collector-artisan Claudia Canestrelli brings back bygone elegance with her repurposed antique earrings, including free-form baroque pearls dangling from gilded bronze cats. (☎340 5776089; Campiello Barbaro 364a; ⏰11am-1pm & 3-5pm Mon & Wed-Sat, 11am-1pm Tue; ⛴Salute)

Le Fórcole di Saverio Pastor

ARTS & CRAFTS

28 Map p56, G4

Only one thing in the world actually moves like Jagger: Mick Jagger's bespoke *fórcola*, hand-carved by Saverio Pastor. Each forked wooden gondola oarlock is individually designed to match a gondolier's height, weight and movement, so the gondola doesn't rock too hard when the gondolier hits a groove. Pastor's miniature *fórcole* twist elegantly, striking an easy balance on gondolas and mantelpieces alike. (☎041 522 56 99; www.forcole.com; Fondamenta Soranzo detta Fornace 341; ⏰8.30am-12.30pm & 2.30-6pm Mon-Sat; ⛴Salute)

Signor Blum

TOYS

29 Map p56, C3

Kids may have to drag adults away from the 2-D wooden puzzles of the Rialto Bridge and grinning wooden duckies before these clever handmade toys induce acute cases of nostalgia. Calder-esque mobiles made of colourful carved gondola prows would seem equally at home in an arty foyer and a nursery. And did we mention the Venice-themed clocks? (☎041 522 63 67; Campo San Barnaba 2840; ⏰9.45am-1.30pm & 2.15-7.15pm Mon-Sat; ⛴Ca' Rezzonico)

Danghyra

CERAMICS

30 Map p56, C2

Spare white bisque cups seem perfect at first glance for a Zen tea ceremony, but look inside – that iridescent lilac glaze is pure Carnevale. Danghyra's striking ceramics are hand-thrown in Venice with a magic touch: her platinum-glazed bowls make the simplest pasta dish appear fit for a modern doge. (☎041 522 41 95; www.danghyra.com; Calle de le Botteghe 3220; ⏰10am-1pm & 3-7pm Tue-Sun; ⛴Ca' Rezzonico)

Ca' Macana (p65)

Acqua Marea

SHOES

31 Map p56, C1

Question: how do you maintain a *bella figura* (good impression) when high tides are sloshing around your ankles? The answer is Martina Ranaldo's delightful rubber boot store, where you can find Wellingtons in lemon yellow and floral prints, ingenious two-tone rubber spats, Meduse ankle boots with coloured soles and comfortable non-leather walking shoes from Cammina Leggero, certified by PETA. (329 1264533; Calle San Pantalon 3750; noon-7pm Mon-Fri; San Tomà)

Papuni Art

JEWELLERY

32 Map p56, C3

Handmade industrial chic isn't what you'd expect to find across the footbridge from baroque Ca' Rezzonico, but Ninfa Salerno's clients delight in the unexpected. The Venetian artisan gives staid pearl strands a sense of humour with bouncy black rubber, weaves fuchsia rubber discs into glowing UFO necklaces, and embeds Murano glass beads in rubber daisy cocktail rings. (041 241 04 34; www.papuniart.it; Ponte dei Pugni 2834a; 11am-7pm Mon & Thu-Sat, 3-7pm Tue & Wed; Ca' Rezzonico)

Explore

San Polo & Santa Croce

Heavenly devotion and earthly delights co-exist in these twinned neighbourhoods, where divine art rubs up against the ancient red-light district, now home to artisan workshops and wine bars. Don't miss Titian's glowing Madonna at I Frari and Tintorettos at Scuola Grande di San Rocco. Grand Canal museums showcase fashion and natural history, while island produce fills the Rialto Market.

The Sights in a Day

Start the morning among masterpieces at **Scuola Grande di San Rocco** (pictured left; p70), then bask in the glow of Titian's Madonna at **I Frari** (p72). Shop backstreet galleries and artisan studios all the way to the **Rialto Market** (p74), where glistening purple octopus and feathery red *radicchio di Treviso* (chicory) present technicolour photo ops.

Having worked up a hunger, follow in-the-know market vendors to **All'Arco** (p82) for some of the city's finest *cicheti* (bar snacks). Fortified, wander west for a lesson in modern Italian art at opulent **Ca' Pesaro** (p80) and then breeze through four centuries of avant-garde fashion, art and perfume at vainglorious **Palazzo Mocenigo** (p80).

As the sun sets take a seat in the *campo* (square) and order from the long list of all-natural wines at **Al Prosecco** (p86) or indulge in a decadent fig and walnut ice cream at **Gelato di Natura** (p84). Wander the maze of Venice's former red-light district to **Antiche Carampane** (p82) for dinner, or get romantic with a concert at the frescoed **Palazetto Bru Zane** (p89).

For a local's day in San Polo, see p76.

Top Sights

Local Life

Best of Venice

Eating

Shopping

Getting There

Vaporetto Most call at Piazzale Roma in Santa Croce. For Santa Croce sights, San Stae, served by lines 1 and N, is most convenient. Lines 1 and N also service Rialto-Mercato and San Tomà in San Polo.

Top Sights
Scuola Grande di San Rocco

You'll swear the paint is still fresh on the 50 action-packed Tintorettos completed between 1575 and 1587 for Scuola Grande di San Rocco, dedicated to the patron saint of the plague-stricken. While the 1575–77 plague claimed one-third of Venice's residents, Tintoretto painted nail-biting scenes of looming despair and last-minute redemption, illuminating a survivor's struggle with breathtaking urgency.

Map p78, B5

041 523 48 64

www.scuolagrandesanrocco.it

Campo San Rocco 3052, San Polo

adult/reduced €10/8

9.30am-5.30pm

San Tomà

Ascension, Tintoretto

Assembly Hall

Downstairs in the assembly hall are works by Venetian A-list artists including Titian, Giorgione and Tiepolo. But Tintoretto steals the show with the story of the Virgin Mary, starting on the left wall with *Annunciation,* where the angel surprises Mary at her sewing. The cycle ends with a dark, cataclysmic *Ascension*, unlike Titian's glowing version at I Frari.

Sala Grande Superiore

Take the grand **Scarpagnino staircase** to the Sala Grande Superiore, where you may be seized with a powerful instinct to duck, given all the action in the **Old Testament ceiling scenes** – you can almost hear the swoop overhead as a winged angel dives to nourish the ailing prophet in *Elijah Fed by an Angel.* Meanwhile, eerie illumination ominously strikes subjects in dark **New Testament wall scenes**. When Tintoretto painted these scenes, the plague had just taken 50,000 Venetians, and the cause of and cure were unknown. With dynamic lines pointing to glimmers of hope on still-distant horizons, Tintoretto created a moving parable for epidemics through the ages.

Sala Albergo

The New Testament cycle ends with the *Crucifixion* in the Sala Albergo, where things suddenly begin to look up – literally. Every Venetian artist who'd survived the plague wanted the commission to paint this building, so Tintoretto cheated a little. Instead of producing sketches like his rival Paolo Veronese, he painted this magnificent *tondo* (ceiling panel) and dedicated it to the saint, knowing that such a gift couldn't be refused, or matched by other artists.

☑ Top Tips

- From spring to late autumn, the artworks provide a bewitching backdrop to top-notch concerts of baroque music. Check the website for details.
- Grab a mirror to avoid neck strain when you view Tintoretto's heroic saints in the ceiling panels.
- A portrait of Tintoretto with his paintbrushes is captured in Francesco Pianta's wooden sculpture. Look upstairs, third from the right beneath Tintoretto's New Testament masterpieces.
- The biggest celebration held in the school is the Feast of San Rocco on 16 August.

Take a Break

Celebrate Venice's survival against the odds with a coffee or *prosecco* at Basegò (p87).

Break for superior gourmet *panini* away from the crowds at Snack Bar Ai Nomboli (p84).

Top Sights
I Frari

As you've no doubt heard, there's a Titian – make that *the* Titian – altarpiece at I Frari. But the 14th-century Italian-brick Gothic basilica is itself a towering achievement, with intricate marquetry choir stalls, a rare Bellini and an eerie Longhena funeral monument. While Canova's white-marble tomb seems permanently moonlit, Titian's *Assunta* seems to shed its own sunlight.

Map p78, C5

041 272 86 18

www.basilicadeifrari.it

Campo dei Frari 3072, San Polo

adult/reduced €3/1.50

9am-6pm Mon-Sat, 1-6pm Sun

San Tomà

Mausoleum of Canova

Assunta

Visitors are inexorably drawn to the front of this cavernous Gothic church by a petite altarpiece that seems to glow from within. This is Titian's 1518 *Assunta* (Ascension), capturing the split second the radiant Madonna reaches heavenward, finds her footing on a cloud, and escapes this mortal coil in a dramatic swirl of Titian-red robes. According to local lore, one glimpse of the Madonna's wrist slipping from her cloak has led many monks to recant their vows over the centuries.

Both inside and outside the painting, onlookers gasp and point at the glorious, glowing sight. Titian outdid himself here, upstaging his own 1526 **Pesaro altarpiece** – a dreamlike composite family portrait of the Holy Family with the Venetian Pesaro family.

Other Masterpieces

As though this weren't quite enough artistic achievement, there's puzzlework marquetry worthy of MC Escher in the **coro** (choir stalls), Bellini's achingly sweet *Madonna with Child* triptych in the **sacristy**, and Bartolomeo Vivarini's *St Mark Enthroned* in the **Capella Corner**.

In the middle of the nave, Baldassare Longhena's **Doge Pesaro funereal monument** is hoisted by four black-marble figures bursting from ragged clothes like Invincible Hulks. Bringing up the rear are disconsolate mourners dabbing at their eyes on Canova's **pyramid mausoleum**, originally intended as a monument to Titian. The great painter was lost to the plague at the age of 90 in 1576, but legend has it that, in light of his contributions here, Venice's strict rules of quarantine were bent to allow Titian's burial near his masterpiece.

☑ Top Tips

- No food is allowed in the church and picture-taking is discouraged. Appropriate dress (eg no shorts, miniskirts, midriff- or tank-tops) is also required.
- Tolling bells give fair warning when the church closes for mass.
- Download a brochure of the basilica or grab a map at the ticket desk for a DIY tour of the incredible range of artworks.
- An audio guide (€2) is available in six languages.
- Atmospheric concerts are occasionally held in the church. Check the website for the schedule.

Take a Break

For lunch seek out cosy Vineria all'Amarone (p88) for hearty plates of gnocchi and a range of Veneto wines.

Top Sights
Rialto Market

Restaurants worldwide are catching on to a secret that this market has loudly touted for 700 years: food tastes better when it's seasonal and local. Before there was a bridge at the Rialto or palaces along the Grand Canal, there was a Pescaria (fish market) and a produce market. So loyal are locals to their market that talk of opening a larger, more convenient mainland fish market was swiftly crushed.

Map p78, H3

041 296 06 58

San Polo

7am-2pm

Rialto-Mercato

Ponte di Rialto

A superb feat of engineering, Antonio da Ponte's 1592 Istrian stone span took three years and 250,000 gold ducats (about €19 million today) to construct. Adorned with stone reliefs depicting St Mark, St Theodore and the Annunciation, the bridge crosses the Grand Canal at its narrowest point, connecting the neighbourhoods of San Polo and San Marco.

Pescaria

Slinging fresh fish for seven centuries and still going strong, the fishmongers of the **Pescaria** (Fish Market; 7am-2pm Tue-Sun) are more vital to Venetian cuisine than any chef. Starting at 7am, they sing the praises of today's catch: mountains of glistening *moscardini* (baby octopus), icebergs of inky *seppie* (cuttlefish) and buckets of crabs, from tiny *moeche* (soft-shell crabs) to *granseole* (spider crabs).

Sustainable fishing practices are not a new idea here; marble plaques show regulations set centuries ago for the minimum allowable sizes for lagoon fish. Seafood tagged 'Nostrana' is locally sourced, and the very best of it is sold at the stall of **Marco Bergamasco** (041 522 53 54; Calle de le Beccarie; 7.30am-noon Tue-Sat), whose clients include Venice's Michelin-starred restaurants.

Produce Market

Veneto *verdure* (vegetables) intrigue with their other-worldy forms, among them Sant'Erasmo *castraure* (baby artichokes), white Bassano asparagus and *radicchio di Treviso* (red, bitter chicory). In the winter, look out for prized *rosa di Gorizia,* a rose-shaped chicory specimen, often eaten raw with honey, vinegar and pancetta in its native region Friuli Venezia Giulia.

Top Tips

- Tuesday and Friday are the best market days; the Pescaria is closed on Monday.
- Gondola rides under the Ponte di Rialto (Rialto Bridge) are romantic, but run to €80 for 30 minutes. For cheap daytime thrills hop the Rialto-Mercato *traghetto* (public gondola) and cross the Grand Canal standing for just €2.
- Note locally sourced fish and produce labelled 'Nostrana', and you'll recognise tasty, sustainable options on dinner menus.
- Explore the surrounding streets for other gourmet food stores selling cheese, wine and regional specialities.

Take a Break

Join thirsty shoppers at cubby-hole Al Mercà (p86) for a chilled glass of Franciacorta.

After they pack up their stalls in the Pescaria, most fishmongers head to All'Arco (p82).

Local Life
Fashion Finds in San Polo

Treasure-hunt through San Polo artisan studios and design boutiques, and find your own signature Venetian style to stand out in any opening-night crowd. From one-of-a-kind paper jewels to custom velvet slippers, Venice's most original fashion statements ensure no one can steal your look – and usually cost less than global brands.

❶ Oh My Blue

Elena Rizzi's beautifully curated **gallery** (041 243 57 41; www.ohmyblue.it; Campo San Tomà 2865; 11am-1pm & 2.30-7.30pm; San Tomà) of contemporary art jewellery and homewares is worthy of a city hosting the most famous art fair in the world. Although Oh My Blue showcases the work of both international and local artists, Elena's Venetian eye for colour, form and texture results in a collection that

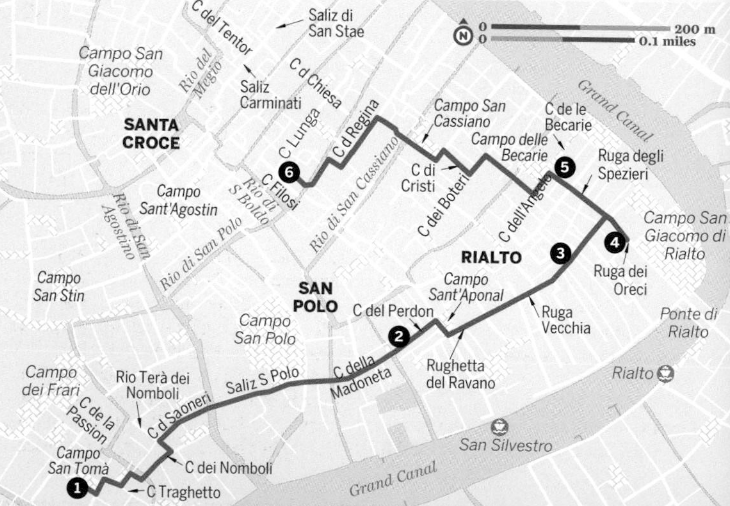

feels uniquely Venetian. Complementing the jewellery is a small collection of glass and homewares, and some iridescent silk clothes.

2 Damocle Edizioni

A meeting point for writers, artists and readers, **Damocle Edizioni** (☎346 8345720; www.edizionidamocle.com; Calle Perdon 1311; ⏲10am-1pm & 3-7pm Mon-Fri, 10am-1pm Sat; ⛴San Silvestro) is both a bijou bookshop and a publishing house, where Pierpaolo Pregnolato produces exquisite multilingual books. Emerging authors, out-of-print classics and rare unpublished works are his stock in trade, each handmade, handstitched book illustrated with original watercolours, woodcuts and even mosaic tesserae.

3 Alberto Sarria

One of the few traditional mask makers left in Venice, **Alberto Sarria** (☎041 520 72 78; www.masksvenice.com; San Polo 777; ⏲10am-7pm; ⛴San Stae) produces creations rendered in watercolour, acrylic and fine gilding, revealing the originality and subtle beauty of a master artisan. Aside from the traditional selection of masquerade and *commedia dell'arte* masks, Alberto also makes delightful marionettes, featuring figures such as Arlecchino and the Bauta Uomo, two notorious characters from Venetian theatre.

4 Pied à Terre

Venetian slippers stay stylish with colourful *furlane* (slippers) at **Pied à Terre** (☎041 528 55 13; www.piedaterre-venice.com; Sotoportego degli Oresi 60; ⏲10am-12.30pm & 2.30-7.30pm; ⛴Rialto-Mercato). Handcrafted with recycled bicycle-tyre treads, they are ideal for finding your footing on a gondola. Choose from velvet, brocade or raw silk in vibrant shades of lemon and ruby. Don't see your size? Shoes can be custom-made and shipped.

5 Murra

Ancient ironwork patterns in Venetian windows inspire the swirling designs on saffron albums and green journals at artisanal **Murra** (☎041 523 40 30; Ruga degli Speziali 299; ⏲10am-7.30pm; ⛴Rialto-Mercato), while the winged lion of St Mark roars with high-fashion fierceness on scarlet handbags and tawny satchels. Designs are handcrafted with incredible precision using hot copper forms.

6 Paperoowl

Stefania Giannici's nimble fingers have been practising origami since she was four years old. Now a master of her craft, she folds, prints, rolls, weaves and handpaints an extraordinary array of paper artworks at **Paperoowl** (☎041 476 19 74; www.paperoowl.com; Calle Seconda del Cristo 2155a; ⏲10.30am-6pm Mon-Fri; ⛴San Silvestro). Must-haves include gorgeous Japanese-style decorative panels, delicate wind chimes inspired by the domes of Venetian churches and chic necklaces that look like Murano glass beads, but cost a fraction of the price.

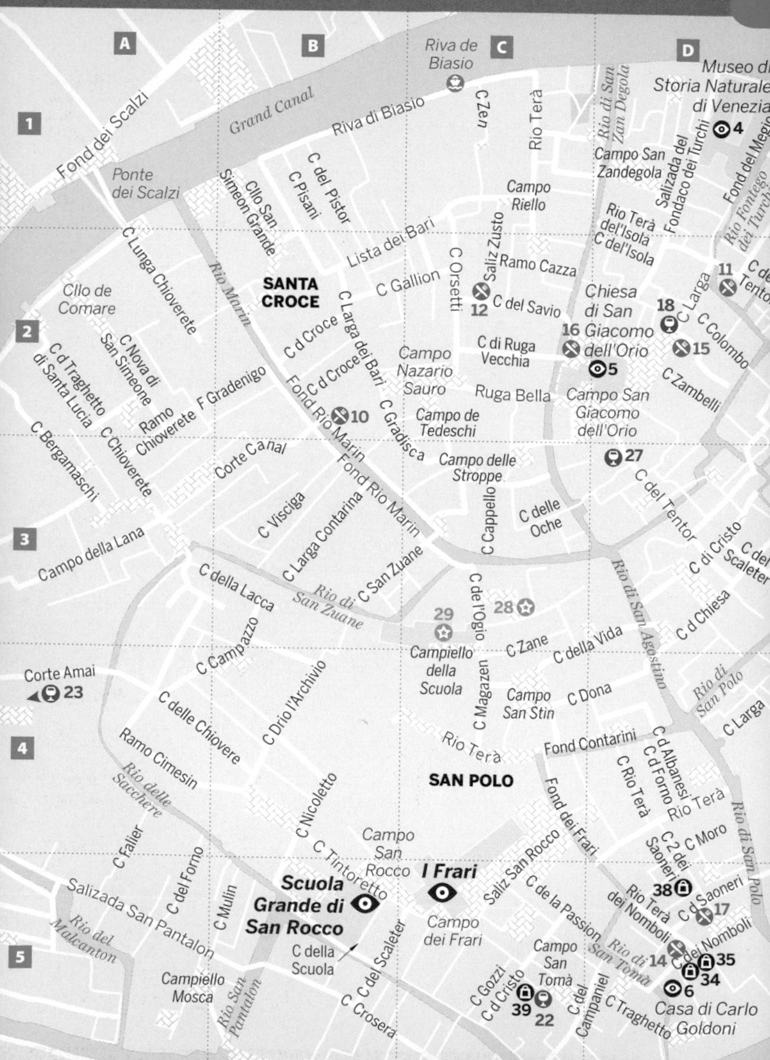

A
B
C
D
1
2
3
4
5
Grand Canal
Riva de Biasio
Riva di Biasio
Fond dei Scalzi
Ponte dei Scalzi
Museo di Storia Naturale di Venezia
4
SANTA CROCE
SAN POLO
Campo San Zandegola
Campo Riello
Chiesa di San Giacomo dell'Orio
5
Campo San Giacomo dell'Orio
Campo Nazario Sauro
Campo de Tedeschi
Campo delle Stroppe
Campiello della Scuola
Campo San Stin
Campo San Rocco
I Frari
Scuola Grande di San Rocco
Campo dei Frari
Campo San Tomà
Casa di Carlo Goldoni
6
Corte Amai
23
10
11
12
14
15
16
17
18
22
27
28
29
34
35
38
39
Rio Marin
Rio di San Zuane
Rio delle Sacchere
Rio del Malcanton
Rio San Pantalon
Rio di San Agostino
Rio di San Polo
Rio di San Tomà
Rio di San Zan Degola
Rio Fontego dei Turchi
Lista dei Bari
Fond Rio Marin
Campo della Lana
Campiello Mosca
Salizada San Pantalon
Fond dei Frari
Fond Contarini
Rio Terà

For reviews see
Top Sights p70
Sights p80
Eating p82
Drinking p86
Entertainment p89
Shopping p89
200 m
0.1 miles
Rialto Market
Ca' Pesaro
Fondazione Prada
Palazzo Mocenigo
CANNAREGIO
RIALTO
SAN MARCO
Grand Canal

Sights

Ca' Pesaro

MUSEUM

1 Map p78, F2

Like a Carnevale costume built for two, the stately exterior of this Baldassare Longhena–designed 1710 *palazzo* hides two intriguing museums: **Galleria Internazionale d'Arte Moderna** and **Museo d'Arte Orientale**. While the former includes art showcased at the Biennale di Venezia, the latter holds treasures from Prince Enrico di Borbone's epic 1887–89 souvenir-shopping spree across Asia. Competing with the artworks are Ca' Pesaro's fabulous painted ceilings, which hint at the power and prestige of the Pesaro clan. (Galleria Internazionale d'Arte Moderna e Museo d'Arte Orientale; 041 72 11 27; www.visitmuve.it; Fondamenta di Ca' Pesaro 2070, Santa Croce; adult/reduced €14/11.50; 10am-6pm Tue-Sun summer, to 5pm winter; San Stae)

Palazzo Mocenigo

MUSEUM

2 Map p78, E2

Venice received a dazzling addition to its property portfolio in 1945 when Count Alvise Nicolò Mocenigo bequeathed his family's 17th-century *palazzo* to the city. While the ground floor hosts temporary exhibitions, the *piano nobile* (main floor) is where you'll find a dashing collection of historic fashion, from duchess *andrienne* (hip-extending dresses) to exquisitely embroidered silk waistcoats. Adding to the glamour and intrigue is an exhibition dedicated to the art of fragrance – an ode to Venice's 16th-century status as Europe's capital of perfume. (041 72 17 98, tour reservations 041 270 03 70; www.visitmuve.it; Salizada di San Stae 1992, Santa Croce; adult/reduced €8/5.50; 10am-5pm Tue-Sun Apr-Oct, to 4pm Nov-Mar; San Stae)

Fondazione Prada

MUSEUM

3 Map p78, F2

This stately Grand Canal palace – designed by Domenico Rossi and completed in 1728 – has been commandeered by Fondazione Prada who are renovating the palace. In between restoration work, Ca' Corner della Regina is the setting for slick temporary exhibitions that explore the art and avant-garde that shape contemporary visual sensibilities. Frescoes on the *piano nobile* (main floor) of the *palazzo* depict Caterina Cornaro, Queen of Cyprus, born in a Gothic building on this very site in 1454. (Ca' Corner; 041 810 91 61; www.fondazioneprada.org; Calle de Ca' Corner 2215, Santa Croce; admission varies; hours vary; San Stae)

Museo di Storia Naturale di Venezia

MUSEUM

4 Map p78, D1

Never mind the doge: insatiable curiosity rules Venice, and inside the Museo di Storia Naturale it runs wild. The adventure begins upstairs with dinosaurs and prehistoric crocodiles, then dashes through evolution to

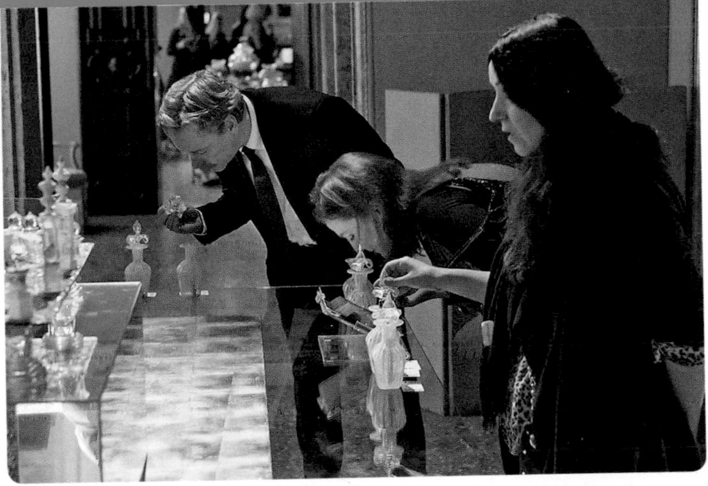

Palazzo Mocenigo fragrance exhibition

Venice's great age of exploration, when adventurers like Marco Polo fetched peculiar specimens from distant lands. (Fondaco dei Turchi, Museum of Natural History; ☎041 275 02 06; www.visitmuve.it; Salizada del Fontego dei Turchi 1730, Santa Croce; adult/reduced €8/5.50; 10am-6pm Tue-Sun Jun-Oct, 9am-5pm Tue-Fri, 10am-6pm Sat & Sun Nov-May; San Stae)

Chiesa di San Giacomo dell'Orio CHURCH

5 Map p78, D2

La Serenissima seems as serene as ever inside the cool gloom of this Romanesque church, founded in the 9th to 10th centuries and completed in Latin-cross form by 1225 with chapels bubbling along the edges. Notable 14th- to 18th-century artworks include luminous **sacristy paintings** by Palma Il Giovane, a rare Lorenzo Lotto *Madonna with Child and Saints,* and an exceptional Veronese crucifix. (www.chorusvenezia.org; Campo San Giacomo dell'Orio 1457, Santa Croce; €3, with Chorus Pass free; 10.30am-4.30pm Mon-Sat; Riva de Biasio)

Casa di Carlo Goldoni MUSEUM

6 Map p78, D5

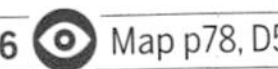

Venetian playwright Carlo Goldoni (1707–93) mastered second and third acts: he was a doctor's apprentice

Understand

Venice's Saving Graces

While the Black Death ravaged the rest of Europe, Venice mounted an inter-faith effort against the plague. The city dedicated a church and *scuola* (religious confraternity) to San Rocco where Venetians could pray for deliverance from the disease, while also consulting resident Jewish and Muslim doctors about prevention measures. Venice established the world's first quarantine zone, with inspections and 40-day waiting periods for incoming ships at Lazaretto. Venice's forward-thinking, inclusive approach created Scuola Grande di San Rocco's artistic masterpieces, which provide comfort to the afflicted and bereaved to this day, and set a public-health standard that has saved countless lives down the centuries.

before switching to law, which proved handy when an *opera buffa* (comic opera) didn't sell. But as the 1st-floor display at his birthplace explains, Goldoni had the last laugh with his social satires. The real highlight here is an 18th-century puppet theatre. (☎041 275 93 25; www.visitmuve.it; Calle dei Nomboli 2794, San Polo; adult/reduced €5/3.50, with Museum Pass free; ⏰10am-5pm Thu-Tue summer, to 4pm winter; San Tomà)

Eating

Antiche Carampane VENETIAN €€€

Hidden in the once shady lanes behind Ponte delle Tette, this culinary indulgence is a trick to find. Once you do, say goodbye to soggy lasagne and hello to a market-driven menu of silky *crudi* (raw fish/seafood), surprisingly light *fritto misto* (fried seafood) and *caramote* prawn salad with seasonal vegetables. Never short of a smart, convivial crowd, it's a good idea to book ahead. (☎041 524 01 65; www.antichecarampane.com; Rio Terà delle Carampane 1911, San Polo; meals €50; ⏰12.45-2.30pm & 7.30-10.30pm Tue-Sat; San Stae)

All'Arco VENETIAN €

Search out this authentic neighbourhood *osteria* (casual tavern) for the best *cicheti* in town. Armed with ingredients from the nearby Rialto Market, father-son team Francesco and Matteo serve miniature masterpieces such as *cannocchia* (mantis shrimp) with pumpkin and roe, and *otrega crudo* (raw butterfish) with mint-and-olive-oil marinade. Even with copious *prosecco,* hardly any meal here tops €20. (☎041 520 56 66; Calle dell'Ochialer 436, San Polo; cicheti from €2; ⏰8am-2.30pm Mon, Tue & Sat, to

7pm Wed-Fri summer, 8am-2.30pm Mon-Sat winter; Rialto-Mercato)

Ristorante Glam

VENETIAN €€€

 Map p78, E1

Step out of your water taxi into the canalside garden of Enrico Bartolini's new Venetian restaurant in the Venart Hotel. Italy's youngest Michelin-starred chef, Bartolini offers a tasting menu focused on local ingredients, pepping up Veneto favourites with unusual spices that would once have graced the tables of this trade-route city. Sommelier Adele Furno supplies the equally excellent wine selection. (Palazzo Venart; 041 523 56 76; www.enricobartolini.net; Calle Tron 1961, Santa Croce; tasting menu €90-110; 12.30-2.30pm & 7.30-10.30pm; San Stae)

Osteria Trefanti

VENETIAN €€

 Map p78, B2

La Serenissima's spice trade lives on at simple, elegant Trefanti, where a dish of marinated prawns, hazelnuts, berries and caramel might get an intriguing kick from garam masala. Furnished with old pews and recycled copper lamps, it's the domain of the competent Sam Metcalfe and Umberto Slongo, whose passion for quality extends to a small, beautifully curated selection of local and organic wines. (041 520 17 89; www.osteriatrefanti.it; Fondamenta Garzotti 888, Santa Croce; meals €40; noon-2.30pm & 7-10.30pm Tue-Sun; San Stae; Riva de Biasio)

Osteria La Zucca

MODERN ITALIAN €€

11 Map p78, D2

With its menu of seasonal vegetarian creations and classic meat dishes, this cosy, woody restaurant consistently hits the mark. Herbs and spices are used to great effect in dishes such as cinnamon-tinged pumpkin flan and chicken curry with yoghurt, lentils and rice. The small interior can get toasty, so reserve canalside seats in summer. (041 524 15 70; www.lazucca.it; Calle del Tentor 1762, Santa Croce; meals €35-40; 12.30-2.30pm & 7-10.30pm Mon-Sat; San Stae)

Antica Besseta

VENETIAN €€

12 Map p78, C2

Wood panelling and fresh flowers set the scene at this veteran trattoria, known for giving contemporary verve to regional classics. The *delizie di pesce dell'Adriatico* – a tasting plate which might see seared scallops served with a brandy and asparagus salsa – makes for a stimulating prologue to dishes like almond-crusted turbot with artichokes. (041 72 16 87; www.anticabesseta.it; Salizada de Cà Zusto 1395, Santa Croce; meals €35; 6.30-10pm Mon, Wed & Thu, noon-2pm & 6.30-10.30pm Fri-Sun; Riva de Biasio)

Dai Zemei

VENETIAN €

 Map p78, G4

Running this closet-sized *cicheti* counter are *zemei* (twins) Franco and Giovanni, who serve loyal regulars small meals with plenty of imagination: gorgonzola lavished with *peperoncino* (chilli) marmalade, duck breast drizzled with truffle oil, or chicory paired with leek and marinated anchovies. A gourmet bargain for inspired bites and impeccable wines – try a crisp *nosiola* or invigorating *prosecco* brut. (041 520 85 96; www.ostariadaizemei.it; Ruga Vecchia San Giovanni 1045, San Polo; cicheti from €1.50; 8.30am-8.30pm Mon-Sat, 9am-7pm Sun; San Silvestro)

Local Life

Talk, Eat, Live Italian

You see a rental sign on a palace door and you start daydreaming: morning banter with the greengrocer, lunchtime gossip at the local *bacaro* (bar), perhaps an evening *ti amo* at a canalside restaurant. There's no doubt that a grasp of Italian will enrich your experience of Venice and enhance your understanding of the city's culture. Luckily for you, **Venice Italian School** (347 9635113, 340 7510863; www.veniceitalianschool.com; Campo San Stin 2504, San Polo; group course 1-/2-weeks €290/530, individual lessons per person €65; San Tomà) is run by Venetians Diego and Lucia Cattaneo, who offer excellent, immersive courses for adults and children between the ages of five and 13 years old.

Snack Bar Ai Nomboli

SANDWICHES €

14 Map p78, D5

This snappy Venetian comeback to McDonald's is never short of local professors, labourers and clued-in out-of-towners. Crusty rolls are packed with local cheeses, fresh greens, roast vegetables, salami, prosciutto and roast beef, and served at an antique marble lunch counter. Beyond standard mayo, condiments range from spicy mustard to wild nettle sauce and fig salsa. Cheap, filling and scrumptious. (041 523 09 95; Rio Terà dei Nomboli 271c, San Polo; sandwiches €2, panini €6; 7am-9pm Mon-Fri, to 3pm Sat; ; San Tomà)

Gelato di Natura

GELATO €

15  Map p78, D2

Along with a dozen other things, Marco Polo is said to have introduced ice cream to Venice after his odyssey to China. At this gelato shop the experimentation continues with vegan versions of your favourite flavours, Japanese rice cakes and the creamiest, small-batch gelato incorporating DOP and IGT accredited local ingredients such as Bronte pistachios, Piedmontese hazelnuts and Amalfi lemons. (340 2867178; www.gelatodinatura.com; Calle Larga 1628, Santa Croce; 1 scoop €1.50; ; Riva di Biasio, San Stae)

Gondolas in front of the Rialto Market (p74)

Il Refolo

PIZZA, ITALIAN €€

16 Map p78, C2

With outdoor tables occupying the *campo* in front of San Giacomo dell'Orio, this is a sunny spot from which to watch gondolas drift by. The food, too, is relaxed and unfussy with a menu offering a range of pizzas, pasta and light seafood dishes. Owned by the Martin family of Michelin-starred Da Fiore; expect top-quality ingredients and standout flavours. (041 524 00 16; Campiello del Piovan 1459, Santa Croce; pizzas €15, meals €35; 7-11pm Tue, noon-2.30pm & 7-11pm Wed-Sun; ; Riva di Biasio, San Stae)

Trattoria da Ignazio

VENETIAN, SEAFOOD €€€

17  Map p78, D5

Dapper white-jacketed waiters serve pristine grilled lagoon fish, fresh pasta and desserts made in-house ('of course') with a proud flourish, on tables bedecked with yellow linen. On cloudy days, homemade crab pasta with a bright Lugana white wine make a fine substitute for sunshine. On sunny days and warm nights, the neighbourhood converges beneath the garden's grape arbour. (041 523 48 52; www.trattoriadaignazio.com; Calle dei Saoneri 2749, San Polo; meals €45-50; noon-3pm & 7-10pm Sun-Fri; San Tomà)

Drinking

Al Prosecco

WINE BAR

18 Map p78, D2

The urge to toast sunsets in Venice's loveliest *campo* is only natural – and so is the wine at Al Prosecco. This forward-thinking bar specialises in *vini naturi* (natural-process wines) – organic, biodynamic, wild-yeast fermented – from enlightened Italian winemakers like Cinque Campi and Azienda Agricola Barichel. So order a glass of unfiltered 'cloudy' *prosecco* and toast to the good things in life. (041 524 02 22; www.alprosecco.com; Campo San Giacomo dell'Orio 1503, Santa Croce; 10am-8pm Mon-Fri, to 5pm Sat Nov-Mar, to 10.30pm Apr-Oct; San Stae)

Al Mercà

WINE BAR

19  Map p78, H3

Discerning drinkers throng to this cupboard-sized counter on a Rialto Market square to sip on top-notch *prosecco* and DOC wines by the glass (from €3). Edibles usually include meatballs and mini *panini* (€1.50), proudly made using super-fresh ingredients. (346 8340660; Campo Cesare Battisti 213, San Polo; 10am-2.30pm & 6-8pm Mon-Thu, to 9.30pm Fri & Sat; Rialto-Mercato)

Do Mori

WINE BAR

20  Map p78, G3

You'll feel like you've stepped into a Rembrandt painting at venerable Do Mori, a dark, rustic bar with roots in the 15th century. Under gleaming, gargantuan copper pots, nostalgists swill one of around 40 wines by the glass, or slurp *prosecco* from old-school champagne saucers. Feeling peckish? Bar bites include pickled onions with anchovies, succulent *polpette* (meatballs) and slices of pecorino. (041 522 54 01; Sotoportego dei do Mori 429, San Polo; 8am-2.30pm & 5-7.30pm Mon-Sat, to 2pm Wed; Rialto-Mercato)

Understand

Grabbing Some Shade

The roots of Venetian bar culture date back at least to the 1700s, when Casanova was frequenting Do Mori. The word *'bacaro'* derives from the name of the Roman wine god Bacchus, and the term *'ombre'* for a glass of wine has its own uniquely Venetian etymology. Whereas in most parts of Italy, *ombre* simply means 'shade' or 'shadows', its slang use in Venice dates back to the days when Venetian wine merchants would set up shop in the shadow of the San Marco bell tower, moving their wares throughout the day to stay out of the sun. In this context, *prendere un'ombra* – 'grab some shade' came to mean 'grab a glass of wine', an affectionate colloquialism that survives to this day.

Cantina Do Spade

BAR

21 Map p78, G3

Famously mentioned in Casanova's memoirs, cosy, brick-lined 'Two Spades' continues to keep Venice in good spirits with its bargain Tri-Veneto wines and young, laid-back management. Come early for market-fresh *fritture* (batter-fried seafood) or linger longer with satisfying, sit-down dishes like *bigoli in salsa* (pasta in anchovy and onion sauce). (041 521 05 83; www.cantinadospade.com; Calle delle Do Spade 860, San Polo; 10am-3pm & 6-10pm; ; Rialto-Mercato)

Basegò

BAR

22 Map p78, C5

Focusing on three essential ingredients – good food, good wine and good music – newly opened Basegò has rapidly formed a dedicated group of drinkers. Indulge in a *cicheti* feast of lagoon seafood, Norcia prosciutto, smoked tuna and Lombard cheeses, and on Friday night enjoy live music from the likes of Alessia Obino and Simone Massaron. (041 850 02 99; www.basego.it; Campo San Tomá, San Polo; 9am-11pm; San Tomà)

Bacareto Da Lele

BAR

23 Map p78, A4

Pocket-sized Da Lele is never short of students and workers, stopping for a cheap, stand-up *ombre* (small glass of wine; from €0.60) on their way to and from the train station. Scan the blackboard for the day's wines and pair them with bite-sized *panini* (€1), stuffed with freshly shaved cured meats and combos like pancetta and artichoke. The place closes for much of August. (Campo dei Tolentini 183, Santa Croce; 6am-8pm Mon-Fri, to 2pm Sat; Piazzale Roma)

Caffè del Doge

CAFE

24 Map p78, G4

Sniff your way to the affable Doge, where dedicated drinkers slurp their way through the menu of speciality imported coffees from Ethiopia to Guatemala, all roasted on the premises. If you're feel especially inspired, you can even pick up a coffee percolator. Add a block of chocolate and you have yourself the perfect pick-me-up. (041 522 77 87; www.caffedeldoge.com; Calle dei Cinque 609, San Polo; 7am-7pm; San Silvestro)

Osteria alla Ciurma

BAR

25 Map p78, G3

This old Rialto storeroom has been converted into a drinking den with a mast holding up the bar and a crew of regulars who come here for a €0.90 glass of house wine and *cicheti* (€1.50) piled high with *baccalà mantecato*. Other top-notch nibbles include courgette flowers stuffed with mozzarella and anchovies and huge plates of marinated seafood, salami or cheese (platters €28). (Calle Galeazza

Prosecco cocktails

406, San Polo; 9am-3pm & 5.30-8.30pm Mon-Sat; Rialto-Mercato)

Vineria all'Amarone

BAR, OSTERIA

26 Map p78, F4

The warm wood-pannelled interior and huge selection of Veneto wines by the glass are just part of the popularity of this friendly bar-cum-restaurant. Other reasons to stop by are the generous *cicheti* platters, the belly-warming plates of gnocchi and braised beef in red wine, and the wine-tasting flights (€27 to €43). Flights include the heady, heavy Amarones from which the bar takes its name. (041 523 11 84; www.allamarone.com; Calle degli Sbianchesini 1131, San Polo; meals €35; 10am-11.45pm Thu-Tue; San Silvestro)

Osteria da Filo

BAR

27 Map p78, D3

Basically a living room where drinks are served, this *osteria* comes complete with creaky sofas, free wi-fi, abandoned novels and the occasional live-music gig. The service can be a little brusque, but the drinks are cheap and the Mediterranean tapas tasty. (Hosteria alla Poppa; 041 524 65 54; www.facebook.com/osteriadafilo; Calle delle Oche 1539, Santa Croce; 4-11pm Mon-Fri, 11am-11pm Sat & Sun; ; Riva de Biasio)

Entertainment

Palazetto Bru Zane

CLASSICAL MUSIC

28 Map p78, C3

Pleasure palaces don't get more romantic than Palazetto Bru Zane, where exquisite harmonies tickle Sebastiano Ricci angels tumbling across stucco-frosted ceilings. Restorations returned the 1695–97 Casino Zane's 100-seat music room to its original function, attracting world-class musicians to enjoy its acoustics from late September to mid-May. (Centre du Musique Romantique Française; 041 521 10 05; www.bru-zane.com; Palazetto Bru Zane 2368, San Polo; adult/reduced €15/5; box office 2.30-5.30pm Mon-Fri, closed late Jul–mid-Aug; San Tomà)

Scuola Grande di San Giovanni Evangelista

OPERA

29 Map p78, C3

Drama comes with the scenery when Italian opera favourites – Puccini's *Tosca,* Verdi's *La Traviata,* Rossini's *Il Barbiere di Seviglia* – are performed in the lavish hall where Venice's secretive Council of Ten socialised. Stage sets can't compare to the scuola: sweep up Mauro Codussi's 15th-century staircase into Giorgio Massari's 1729 hall, and take your seat amid Giandomenico Tiepolo paintings. (041 426 65 59; www.scuolasangiovanni.it; Campiello della Scuola 2454, San Polo; adult/reduced from €20/5; San Tomà)

La Casa Del Cinema

CINEMA

30 Map p78, E2

Venice's public film archive shows art films in a modern 50-seat, wood-beamed screening room inside Palazzo Mocenigo (p80). Original-language classics are shown Monday and Thursday, while first-run independent films are screened on Friday; check online for pre-release previews and revivals with introductions by directors, actors and scholars. (Videoteca Pasinetti; 041 274 71 40; www.comune.venezia.it/cinema; Salizada San Stae 1990, Santa Croce; annual membership adult/reduced €35/25; 9am-1pm & 3-10pm Mon-Fri; San Stae)

Shopping

Veneziastampa

ARTS & CRAFTS

31 Map p78, E3

Mornings are best to catch the 1930s Heidelberg machine in action, but whenever you arrive, you'll find mementos hot off the proverbial press. Veneziastampa recalls more elegant times, when postcards were gorgeously lithographed and Casanovas invited dates upstairs to 'look at my etchings'. Pick your signature symbols – meteors, faucets, trapeze artists – for original bookplates and cards. (041 71 54 55; www.veneziastampa.com; Campo Santa Maria Mater Domini 2173, Santa Croce; 8.30am-7.30pm Mon-Fri, 9am-12.30pm Sat; San Stae)

Drogheria Mascari

FOOD & DRINKS

32 Map p78, G3

Ziggurats of cayenne, leaning towers of star anise and chorus lines of olive oils draw awestruck foodies to Mascari's windows. Indoors, chefs clutch truffle jars like holy relics, kids ogle candy in copper-lidded jars and dazed gourmands confront 50 different aromatic honeys. For small-production Italian *vino* – including Veneto cult producers like Giuseppe Quintarelli – don't miss the backroom *cantina*. (041 522 97 62; www.imascari.com; Ruga degli Spezieri 381, San Polo; 8am-1pm & 4-7.30pm Mon, Tue & Thu-Sat, 8am-1pm Wed; Rialto-Mercato)

Gmeiner

SHOES

33 Map p78, G4

Paris, London, Venice: Gabriele Gmeiner honed her shoemaking craft at Hermès and John Lobb, and today jet-setters fly to Venice just for her ultra-sleek Oxfords with hidden 'bent' seams and her minutely hand-stiched brogues, made to measure for men and women (around €3000, including hand-carved wooden last). (338 896 21 89; www.gabrielegmeiner.com; Campiello del Sol 951, San Polo; by appointment 9am-1pm & 3-7pm Mon-Fri; Rialto-Mercato)

Sabbie e Nebbie

GIFTS & SOUVENIRS

34 Map p78, E4

East–West trade-route trends begin here, with chic cast-iron teapots, Japanese-textile patchwork totes, and Orient-inspired ceramics by Rita Menardi. Trained in design and graphics, owner Maria Teresa Laghi has a sharp eye for beautiful, unique and inspiring objects, making her shop especially popular with discerning locals. (041 71 90 73; www.sabbienebbie.com; Calle dei Nomboli 2768a, San Polo; 10am-12.30pm & 4-7.30pm Mon-Sat; San Tomà)

Franco Furlanetto

ARTS & CRAFTS

35 Map p78, D5

Masks and violins inspire Franco's designs for *forcole* (gondola oarlocks) and *remi* (oars), hand-carved on-site from blocks of walnut, cherry and pear wood. There's a science to each creation, perfectly weighted and angled to propel a vessel forward, but also a delicate art. For its sculptural finesse, Franco's work has been shown in New York's Metropolitan Museum of Art. (041 520 95 44; www.ffurlanetto.com; Calle delle Nomboli 2768, San Polo; 10am-6pm Mon-Fri, to 5pm Sat; San Tomà)

Casa del Parmigiano

FOOD

36 Map p78, H3

Suitably set beside the appetite-piquing Rialto Market, cheery Casa del Parmigiano heaves with coveted cheeses from potent *parmigiano reggiano* aged three years, to rare, local Asiago Stravecchio di Malga. All

Understand

Venice's 'Honest Courtesans'

The Age of Decadence

With trade revenues and the value of the Venetian ducat slipping in the 16th century, Venice's fleshpots brought in far too much valuable foreign currency to be outlawed. Instead, Venice opted for regulation and taxation. Rather than baring all in the rough-and-ready streets around the Rialto, prostitutes could only display their wares from the waist up in windows, or sit bare-legged on window sills. Venice decreed that to distinguish themselves from noblewomen who increasingly dressed like them, ladies of the night should ride in gondolas with red lights. By the end of the 16th century, the town was flush with some 12,000 registered prostitutes, creating a literal red-light district.

Education Pays

Venice's *cortigiane oneste* were no ordinary strumpets. An 'honest courtesan' earned the title not by offering a fair price, but by providing added value with style and wit that reflected well on her patrons. They were not always beautiful or young, but *cortigiane oneste* were well educated, dazzling their admirers with poetry, music and apt social critiques. In the 16th century, some Venetian families spared no expense on their daughters' educations: beyond an advantageous marriage, educated women who become *cortigiane oneste* could command prices 60 times those of a *cortigiana di lume* ('courtesan of the lamp' – streetwalker).

An Alternative Guidebook

A catalogue of 210 of Venice's *piu honorate cortigiane* (most honoured courtesans) was published in 1565, listing contact information and rates, payable directly to the courtesan's servant, her mother or, occasionally, her husband. A *cortigiana onesta* might circulate in Venetian society as the known mistress of one or more admirers, who compensated her for her company rather than services rendered. Syphilis was an occupational hazard, and special hospices were founded for infirm courtesans.

Veneziastampa (p89)

are kept good company by fragrant cured meats, *baccalà* (cod) and trays of marinated Sicilian olives. Drooling? (041 520 65 25; www.aliani-casadelparmigiano.it; Campo Cesare Battisti 214, San Polo; 8am-1.30pm Mon-Wed, to 7.30pm Thu-Sat; Rialto-Mercato)

Cárte

ARTS & CRAFTS

37 Map p78, F3

Venice's shimmering lagoon echoes in marbled-paper earrings and artist's portfolios, thanks to the steady hands and restless imagination of *carta marmorizzata* (marbled-paper) *maestra* Rosanna Corrò. After years restoring ancient Venetian books, Rosanna began creating her original, bookish beauties: tubular statement necklaces, op-art jewellery boxes, one-of-a-kind contemporary handbags, and even wedding albums. (320 0248776; www.cartevenezia.it; Calle dei Cristi 1731, San Polo; 10.30am-5.30pm; Rialto-Mercato)

Gilberto Penzo

ARTS & CRAFTS

38 Map p78, D5

Yes, you actually can take a gondola home in your pocket. Anyone fascinated by the models at the Museo Storico Navale (p119) will go wild here, amid handmade wooden models of Venetian boats, including some that are seaworthy (or at least bathtub worthy). Signor Penzo also creates kits, so crafty types and kids can have a crack at it themselves. (041 71 93 72; www.veniceboats.com; Calle 2 dei Saoneri 2681, San Polo; 9am-1pm & 3-6pm Mon-Sat; San Tomà)

Il Baule Blu

VINTAGE

39 Map p78, C5

A curiosity cabinet of elusive treasures where you can expect to stumble across anything from 1970s bubble sunglasses and vintage Murano *murrine* (glass beads) to vintage Italian coats and frocks in good condition. If travel has proved tough on your kid's favourite toy, first aid and kind words will be administered at the in-house teddy hospital. (041 71 94 48; Campo San Tomà 2916a, San Polo; 10.30am-12.30pm & 4-7.30pm Mon-Sat; San Tomà)

Emilio Ceccato

CLOTHING

40 Map p78, H4

If you've been eyeing up the natty striped T-shirts, devilishly soft winter wool hats and crepe pants sported by Venice's gondoliers then make a beeline for official supplier Emilio Ceccato. Here you'll find a huge selection of shirts, pants and jackets all emblazoned with the gondoliers logo. What's more, proceeds from purchases are reinvested in training programs and boatyards. (041 522 27 00; www.emilioceccato.com; Sotoportego degli Oresi 16-17, San Polo; 10am-1.30pm & 2.30-7pm Mon-Sat, from 11am Sun; Rialto-Mercato)

Bottega Orafa ABC

JEWELLERY

41 Map p78, E2

Master of metals, Andrea d'Agostino takes his influence from the Japanese technique of *mokume gane* (meaning 'metal with woodgrain'), masterful examples of which are on display in the Asian gallery of Ca' Pesaro (p80). The result is rings, pendants and bracelets with swirling multicoloured patterns that seem to capture the dappled lagoon waters for all time in silver and gold. (041 524 40 01; www.orafaabc.com; Calle del Tentor 1839, Santa Croce; 9.30am-1pm & 3.30-7.30pm Tue-Sat; San Stae)

Explore

Cannaregio & the Ghetto

Anyone could adore Venice on looks alone, but in Cannaregio you'll fall for its personality. A few streets over from bustling Strada Nova is the Ghetto, a living monument to the outsized contributions of Venice's Jewish community. Between the art-filled Madonna dell'Orto and the Renaissance beauty of Santa Maria dei Miracoli are some of Venice's top *cicheti* (Venetian tapas) bars and neighbourhood restaurants.

The Sights in a Day

The Strada Nova, created in 1871 by filling in canals, slices through Cannaregio. From this pedestrian highway you can reach all of the area's finest churches: the miraculous, all-marble **Chiesa di Santa Maria dei Miracoli** (p102); bombastic, baroque **I Gesuiti** (p103); and **Chiesa della Madonna dell'Orto** (p102), the neighbourhood church of famous local Tintoretto, which is bedecked with his masterpieces.

After such a divine start, take a seat on sunny Fondamenta de la Misericordia at **Vino Vero** (p99) for gourmet *cicheti* and *pizzetta* and superior glasses of wine. Then hop across the tiny bridge to **the Ghetto** (p96), the heart of Venice's segregated Jewish community. Refuel with a sweet ground-almond *impade* at kosher bakery **Panificio Volpe Giovanni** (p106) before discovering Grand Canal photo ops and stolen masterpieces inside **Ca' d'Oro** (p102).

Take a leaf out of the locals hand book and down tools for canalside *aperitivo* at **Timon** (p99), **Al Parlamento** (p98) and **Dodo Caffè** (p109). You could spend the whole night drinking in the romantic scene, but dinner at **Osteria da Rioba** (p105) with its Sant'Erasmo-sourced ingredients is worth surrendering your seat for.

For a local's day in Cannaregio, see p98.

Top Sights

Local Life

Best of Venice

Getting There

Vaporetto After Ferrovia, there are two Grand Canal stops: San Marcuola (lines 1 and 2) and Ca' d'Oro (1). Lines 4.1, 4.2, 5.1 and 5.2 go from Ferrovia to Fondamente Nove. Line 3 goes to Murano. From Fondamente Nove, lines 12 and 13 go to the northern islands.

Top Sights
Campo del Ghetto Nuovo & the Ghetto

This Cannaregio corner once housed a *getto* (foundry) – but its role as Venice's designated Jewish quarter from the 16th to 19th centuries gave the word a whole new meaning. From 1516 onwards, Jewish artisans and lenders tended to Venice's commercial enterprises by day, while at night and on Christian holidays they were restricted to the gated island of Ghetto Nuovo.

Map p100, C3

Guglie

Passageway leading into the Ghetto

Museo Ebraico

At the Ghetto's heart, the **Museo Ebraico** (Jewish Museum; ☎041 71 53 59; www.museoebraico.it; Campo del Ghetto Nuovo 2902b; adult/reduced €8/6, incl tour €12/10; ⊙10am-7pm Sun-Fri Jun-Sep, to 5.30pm Sun-Fri Oct-May) explores the history of Venice's Jewish community through everyday artefacts, including finely wrought devotional objects and books published in the Ghetto during the Renaissance.

The Synagogues

As you enter **Campo del Ghetto Nuovo,** look up: atop private apartments is the wooden cupola of the starkly beautiful 1575 **Schola Italiana** (Italian Synagogue; ⊙entry by guided tour via Museo Ebraico), the poorest Jewish community in the Ghetto.

Also recognisable from the square by its five long windows, the **Schola Tedesca** (German Synagogue; ⊙entry by guided tour via Museo Ebraico) has been the spiritual home of Venice's rich Ashkenazi community since 1528. The baroque pulpit and carved benches downstairs are topped by a gilded, elliptical women's gallery, modelled after a Venetian opera balcony.

In the corner of the *campo* is the wooden cupola of the **Schola Canton** (Corner Synagogue; ⊙entry by guided tour via Museo Ebraico), built c 1531 with gilded rococo interiors added in the 18th century.

Over the bridge in **Campo del Ghetto Vecchio**, Sephardic Jewish refugees raised two synagogues with 17th-century interiors attributed to Baldassare Longhena. **Schola Levantina** (Levantine Synagogue) has a magnificent woodworked pulpit, while the **Schola Spagnola** (Spanish Synagogue; ⊙entry by guided tour via Museo Ebraico) has exuberant marble and carved-wood baroque interiors.

☑ Top Tips

▶ Although you can stroll around this peaceful precinct day and night, the best way to truly experience the Ghetto is to take one of the guided synagogue tours offered by the Museo Ebraico, departing hourly from 10.30am.

▶ For information about local Jewish life, call into the **Jewish Community Info Point** (☎041 523 75 65; www.jvenice.org; Calle Ghetto Vecchio 1222; ⊙9.30am-5pm Mon-Fri).

✗ Take a Break

Ghetto Vecchio is home to one of Venice's best bakeries, Panificio Volpe Giovanni (p106) – and it's kosher too!

The canal to the north of the Ghetto Nuovo has arguably the best strip of *cicheti* bars in Venice. Our favourite is Vino Vero (p99).

Local Life
Cannaregio's Cicheti Circuit

After lavish canalside Cannaregio lunches, skip three-course dinners and make meals of *cicheti* (Venetian tapas) instead. Platters appear on counters across Cannaregio at 6pm, from perfect *polpette* (meatballs) to top-notch *crudi* (Venetian-style sashimi, laced with olive oil and/or aged balsamic vinegar). For bargain gourmet adventures, graze these Cannaregio *cicheti* hot spots.

1 Tramezzini & DJs at Al Parlamento

Entire university careers and international romances are owed to the powerful espresso, 6pm-to-9pm happy-hour cocktails and excellent overstuffed *tramezzini* (triangular stacked sandwiches) at **Al Parlamento** (041 244 02 14; www.facebook.com/alParlamento; Fondamenta Savorgnan 511; 7.30am-1.30am; ; Crea). Draped ship ropes accentuate the

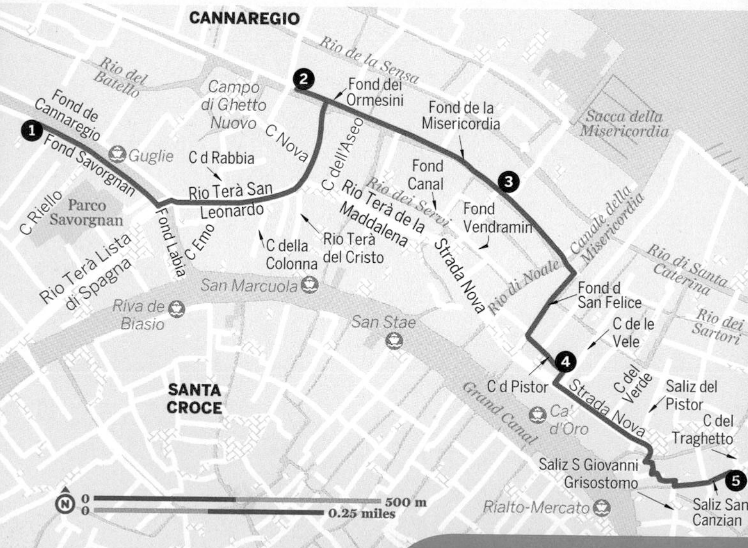

canal views from the large windows at the front. Drop by in the evening and you might catch a live band or DJ set.

❷ Crostini & Concerts at Timon

Find a spot on the boat moored along the canal at **Timon** (☎041 524 60 66; Fondamenta dei Ormesini 2754; ⏰6pm-1am; ⛴San Marcuola) and watch the parade of drinkers and dreamers arrive for seafood *crostini* (open-faced sandwiches) and quality organic and DOC wines by the *ombre* (half-glass) or carafe. Folk singers play sets canal-side when the weather obliges; when it's cold, regulars scoot over to make room for newcomers at indoor tables.

❸ More Crostini at Vino Vero

Lining the exposed brick walls of **Vino Vero** (☎041 275 00 44; www.facebook.com/vinoverovenezia; Fondamenta de la Misericordia 2497; ⏰11am-midnight Tue-Sun, from 6pm Mon; ⛴San Marcuola) are interesting small-production wines, including a great selection of natural and biodynamic labels. However it's the *cicheti* that really lifts this place beyond the ordinary, with arguably the most mouth-watering display of continually replenished, fresh *crostini* in the entire city. In the evenings the crowd spills out onto the canal.

❹ Meatballs & Ombre at Osteria Alla Vedova

Culinary convictions run deep here at one of Venice's oldest **osterie** (☎041 528 53 24; Calle del Pistor 3912; meals €28-30; ⏰11.30am-2.30pm & 6.30-10.30pm Mon-Wed, Fri & Sat, 6.30-10.30pm Sun; ⛴Ca' d'Oro), so you won't find *spritz* (*prosecco* cocktails) or coffee on the menu or pay more than €2 to snack on a Venetian meatball. Enjoy superior seasonal *cicheti* and *ombre* with the local crowd at the bar, or call ahead for table service and strictly authentic Venetian dishes.

❺ Sarde in Saor at Un Mondo di Vino

Get here early for first crack at marinated artichokes and *sarde in saor* (sardines in tangy onion marinade) and claim a few square inches of ledge for your plate and wineglass. **Un Mondo di Vino** (☎041 521 10 93; www.unmondodivinovenezia.com; Salizada San Canzian 5984a; ⏰11am-3pm & 5.30-11pm Tue-Sun; ⛴Rialto) offers dozens of wines by the glass, so take a chance on a weird blend or obscure varietal.

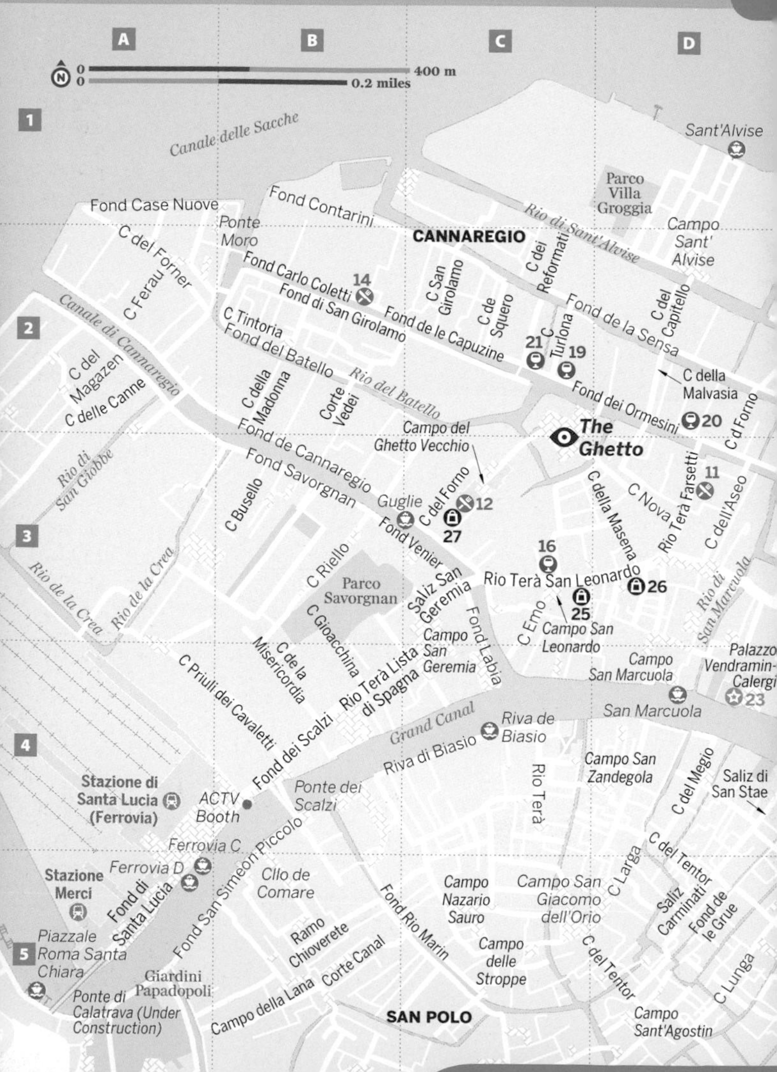
A
B
C
D
1
2
3
4
5
0
400 m
0
0.2 miles
Canale delle Sacche
Sant'Alvise
Parco Villa Groggia
Fond Case Nuove
Fond Contarini
Ponte Moro
CANNAREGIO
Rio di Sant'Alvise
Campo Sant' Alvise
C del Forner
Fond Carlo Coletti
14
Fond di San Girolamo
C San Girolamo
C de Squero
C dei Reformati
C Turlona
Fond de la Sensa
C del Capitello
C Ferau
Canale di Cannaregio
C Tintoria
Fond del Batello
Fond de le Capuzine
21
19
C della Malvasia
C del Magazen
C delle Canne
C della Madonna
Corte Vedei
Rio del Batello
Fond dei Ormesini
20
C d Forno
Campo del Ghetto Vecchio
The Ghetto
Rio di San Giobbe
Fond de Cannaregio
Fond Savorgnan
C Busello
Guglie
C del Forno
12
27
C della Masena
C Nova
Rio Terà Farsetti
11
C dell'Aseo
Fond Venier
16
Rio de la Crea
C Riello
Parco Savorgnan
Saliz San Geremia
Rio Terà San Leonardo
26
25
Rio di San Marcuola
C Gioacchina
Fond Labia
C Emo
Campo San Leonardo
C de la Misericordia
Campo San Geremia
Rio Terà Lista di Spagna
Campo San Marcuola
Palazzo Vendramin-Calergi
23
C Priuli dei Cavaletti
San Marcuola
Grand Canal
Riva de Biasio
Fond dei Scalzi
Riva di Biasio
Rio Terà
Campo San Zandegola
C del Megio
Saliz di San Stae
Stazione di Santa Lucia (Ferrovia)
ACTV Booth
Ponte dei Scalzi
Fond San Simeon Piccolo
Ferrovia C
Ferrovia D
Stazione Merci
Fond di Santa Lucia
Cllo de Comare
Fond Rio Marin
Campo Nazario Sauro
Campo San Giacomo dell'Orio
C Larga
C del Tentor
Saliz Carminati
Fond de le Grue
Piazzale Roma Santa Chiara
Ramo Chioverete
Campo delle Stroppe
C del Tentor
Giardini Papadopoli
Corte Canal
C Lunga
Ponte di Calatrava (Under Construction)
Campo della Lana
SAN POLO
Campo Sant'Agostin

E
F
G
H
1
2
3
4
5
For reviews see
Top Sights p96
Sights p102
Eating p105
Drinking p107
Entertainment p109
Shopping p110
Rio degli Zecchini
Orto
Fond Madonna de l'Orto
Campiello Piave
Chiesa della Madonna dell'Orto
3
Campo de la Madonna de l'Orto
Rio della Madonna dell'Orto
Fond Gasparo Contarini
C dei Mori
Rio de la Sensa
10
C Larga
6
C Tintoretto
22
Rio dei Muti
Corte Vecchia
Sacca della Misericordia
Canale delle Fondamente Nuove
Rio della Misericordia
Fond dell'Abbazia
Fond Canal
15
C Zancani
Fond de la Misericordia
Canale della Misericordia
C Longa Santa Caterina
Fond Nove
C Marco Foscarini
Saliz dei Specchieri
4
I Gesuiti
C de le Tre Crose
Fondamente Nove B
Fond Santa Caterina
Fond Zen
Campo dei Gesuiti
Rio dei Gesuiti
Rio della Maddalena
Strada Nova
Rio di Noale
Fond di San Felice
C de la Raccheta
Rio de la Raccheta
Fallani Venezia
5
C Larga dei Botteri
Saliz Seriman
C Venier
C Priuli
Rio di Santa Sofia
R Due Pozzi
C de le Vele
Rio Terà Barba Frutarol
C Spezier
C del Volto
C Cordoni
C del Fumo
Rio de la Panada
San Stae
17
C di Ca' d'Oro
Campo San Stae
Galleria Giorgio Franchetti alla Ca' d'Oro
2
C del Pistor
C del Verde
Rio Terà d Franceschi
18
24
28
C Widman
Rio Terà dei Birri
C del Squero
Rio dei Mendicanti
Fond dei Mendicanti
Fond Rimpetto Mocenigo
Ca' d'Oro
Strada Nova
13
Campo Santa Sofia
8
9
Campo dei SS Apostoli
Campiello della Cason
Campo Santa Maria Nova
7
C d Testa
Fond de l'Ogio
C d Regina
Rio dei Santi Apostoli
Chiesa di Santa Maria dei Miracoli
1
C Larga G Gallina
Campo SS Giovanni e Paolo
Campo San Cassiano
Campo delle Becarie
Rialto-Mercato
Campo dei Miracoli
C Castelli
RIALTO
Campo San Giacomo di Rialto
CASTELLO

Sights

Chiesa di Santa Maria dei Miracoli

CHURCH

1 Map p100, G5

When Nicolò di Pietro's *Madonna* icon started miraculously weeping in its outdoor shrine around 1480, crowd control became impossible. With public fundraising and marble scavenged from San Marco slag heaps, this magnificent church was built (1481–89) to house the painting. Pietro and Tullio Lombardo's design dropped grandiose Gothic in favour of human-scale harmonies, introducing Renaissance church architecture to Venice. (Campo dei Miracoli 6074; adult/reduced €3/1.50, with Chorus Pass free; 10.30am-4.30pm Mon-Sat; Fondamente Nove)

Local Life

Painting Venice

Sign up for a session at **Painting Venice** (340 544 52 27; www.paintingvenice.com; Cannaregio; 2hr private lessons €100, 2-day workshops €280) with professionally trained and practising artists Caroline, Sebastien and Katrin and you'll strike out into tranquil *campi* (squares) in the tradition of classic Venetian *vedutisti* (outdoor artists). Beginners learn the basic concepts of painting 'en plein air', while those with more advanced skills receive tailormade tuition. It's a great way to slow down and really appreciate the colour and composition of each view.

Galleria Giorgio Franchetti alla Ca' d'Oro

MUSEUM

2 Map p100, F4

One of the most beautiful buildings on the Grand Canal, 15th-century Ca' d'Oro's lacy arcaded Gothic facade is resplendent even without the original gold-leaf details that gave the palace its name (Golden House). Baron Franchetti (1865–1922) bequeathed this treasure-box palace to Venice, packed with his collection of masterpieces, many of which were originally plundered from Veneto churches during Napoleon's conquest of Italy. The baron's ashes are interred beneath an ancient purple porphyry column in the magnificent open-sided, mosaic-floored court downstairs. (041 520 03 45; www.cadoro.org; Calle di Ca' d'Oro 3932; adult/reduced €8.50/4.25; 8.15am-2pm Mon, to 7.15pm Tue-Sun; Ca' d'Oro)

Chiesa della Madonna dell'Orto

CHURCH

3 Map p100, E2

This elegantly spare 1365 brick Gothic church remains one of Venice's best-kept secrets. It was the parish church of Venetian Renaissance painter Tintoretto (1518–94), who filled the church with his paintings and is buried in the chapel to the right of the altar. (Campo de la Madonna

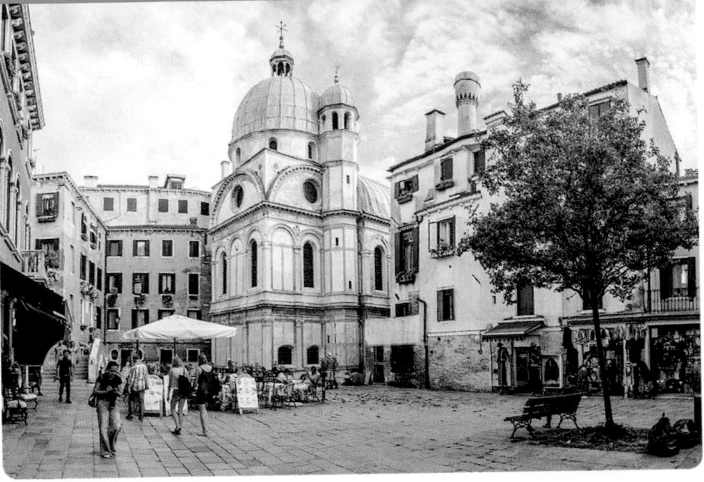

Chiesa di Santa Maria dei Miracoli

de l'Orto 3520; adult/reduced €3/2; 10am-5pm Mon-Sat; Orto)

I Gesuiti CHURCH

 Map p100, G3

Giddily over the top even by rococo standards, this glitzy 18th-century Jesuit church is difficult to take in all at once, with staggering white-and-green intarsia (inlaid marble) walls that look like a version of Venetian flocked wallpaper, marble curtains draped over the pulpit and a marble carpet spilling down the altar stairs. While the ceiling is a riot of gold-and-white stuccowork, some gravity is provided by Titian's uncharacteristically gloomy *Martyrdom of St Lawrence,* on the left as you enter the church. (Santa Maria Assunta; 041 528 65 79; Salizada dei Specchieri 4882; €1; 10am-noon & 3.30-5.30pm; Fondamente Nove)

Fallani Venezia ART

 Map p100, G4

Fiorenzo Fallani's laboratory has been credited with transforming screenprinting from a medium of reproduction to an innovative and creative artistic technique. Courses get you from printing your own T-shirt to more complex processes using different colours, acetates and frames. Even if you don't fancy taking a course, this is a great place to

Understand

Venetian Jewish History

Renaissance in the Ghetto

During the 14th- to 16th-century Italian Renaissance, pragmatic Venice granted Jewish communities the right to practise certain professions key to the city's livelihood, including medicine, trade, banking, fashion and publishing. Despite a 10-year censorship order issued by the Church in Rome in 1553, Jewish Venetian publishers contributed hundreds of titles popularising new Renaissance ideas on humanist philosophy, medicine and religion – including the first printed Qur'an.

Interfaith Enlightenment

Leading thinkers of all faiths flocked to Ghetto literary salons. In the 17th century, the Schola Italiana's learned rabbi Leon da Modena was so widely respected that Christians attended his services. When Venetian Jewish philosopher Sara Copia Sullam (1592–1641) was anonymously accused of denying the immortality of the soul – a heresy punishable by death under the Inquisition – Sullam responded with a treatise on immortality written in two days. The manifesto became a bestseller, and Sullam's writings are key works of early modern Italian literature.

Signs of Restriction

On the wall at No 1131 Calle del Ghetto Vecchio, an official 1704 decree of the Republic forbids Jews converted to Christianity entry into the Ghetto, punishable by 'the rope [hanging], prison, galleys, flogging...and other greater punishments, depending on the judgment of their excellencies (the Executors Against Blasphemy)'. Such restrictions on Venice's Jewish community were abolished under Napoleon in 1797, when some 1626 Ghetto residents gained standing as Venetian citizens.

The Enduring Legacy

Mussolini's 1938 Racial Laws revived discriminatory rules, and in 1943 most Jewish Venetians were deported to concentration camps. As a memorial on the northeast end of the Campo del Ghetto Nuovo notes, only 37 returned. Today few of Venice's 400-person Jewish community actually live in the Ghetto, but its legacy remains in bookshops, art galleries and religious institutions.

purchase original art prints of Venice. (☎041 523 57 72; www.fallanivenezia.com; Salizada Seriman 4875; 1/4/8hr courses €40/100/200; Fondamente Nove)

Eating

Osteria da Rioba VENETIAN €€€

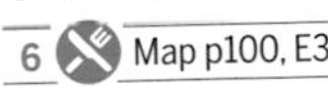

6 Map p100, E3

Taking the lead with fresh seafood and herbs pulled from the family's Sant'Erasmo farm, Da Rioba's inventive kitchen turns out exquisite plates as colourful and creative as the artwork on the walls. This is prime date-night territory. In winter, cosy up in the wood-beamed interior; in summer sit canalside. Reservations recommended. (☎041 524 43 79; www.darioba.com; Fondamenta de la Misericordia 2553; meals €46-49; 12.30-2.30pm & 7.30-11pm Tue-Sun; Orto)

Osteria Boccadoro VENETIAN €€€

7 Map p100, H5

Birds sweetly singing in this *campo* are probably angling for your leftovers, but they don't stand a chance. Chef-owner Luciano's creative *crudi* (raw seafood) are two-bite delights and cloudlike gnocchi and homemade pasta is gone entirely too soon. Save room for luxuriant desserts. (☎041 521 10 21; www.boccadorovenezia.it; Campiello Widmann 5405a; meals €40-55; noon-3pm & 7-10pm Tue-Sun; Fondamente Nove)

Ai Promessi Sposi VENETIAN €€

8 Map p100, F5

Bantering Venetians thronging the bar are the only permanent fixtures at this neighbourhood *osteria* (casual tavern), where ever-changing menus feature fresh Venetian seafood and Veneto meats at excellent prices. Seasonal standouts include *seppie in umido* (cuttlefish in rich tomato sauce) and housemade pasta, but pace yourself for cloudlike tiramisu and excellent semifreddo. (☎041 241 27 47; Calle d'Oca 4367; meals €29-37; 6.30-11.30pm Mon & Wed, 11.30am-3pm & 6.30-11.30pm Tue & Thu-Sun; Ca' d'Oro)

Trattoria da Bepi Già "54" VENETIAN €€

9 Map p100, G5

Much better than it looks from the outside, Da Bepi is a traditional trattoria in the very best sense. The interior is a warm, wood-panelled cocoon, and the service is efficient and friendly. Take their advice on the classic Venetian menu and order *spaghetti col nero di seppia* (with cuttlefish ink), grilled fish and a tiramisu that doesn't disappoint. (☎041 528 50 31; www.dabepi.it; Campo SS Apostoli 4550; meals €24-37; noon-3pm & 7-10pm Fri-Wed; Ca' d'Oro)

Osteria L'Orto dei Mori

ITALIAN **€€€**

10 Map p100, E3

Not since Tintoretto lived next door has this neighbourhood seen so much action, thanks to this bustling *osteria*. Sicilian chef Lorenzo makes fresh pasta daily, including squid atop *tagliolini*. Fish-shaped lamps set a playful mood in an upmarket space. (041 524 36 77; www.osteriaortodeimori.com; Campo dei Mori 3386; meals €46-51; 12.30-3.30pm & 7pm-midnight Wed-Mon; Orto)

Local Life

Adventures in Wine & Cicheti

Prosecco, Soave and Amarone aren't the only wines in town. Expand your happy-hour options on a unique Cichetto Row with **Row Venice** (347 7250637; www.rowvenice.org; Fondamenta Gasparo Contarini; 90min lessons 1-2 people €85, 3/4 people €120/140; Orto). This gentle 2½-hour row bar-hops between Cannaregio's canalside bars (€240 for two people) with handy instructions on Veneto varieties and *voga* (Venetian rowing). The outfit also offers lessons on rowing a traditional *batellina coda di gambero* (shrimp-tailed boat) standing up like gondoliers do.

Landlubbers in search of a good backstreet *bacaro* (bar) crawl, should opt for fun and informed tours with Monica Cesarato from **Cook in Venice** (www.cookinvenice.com; tours €35-60, courses €185-225).

Cantina Aziende Agricole

VENETIAN **€**

11  Map p100, D3

For over 40 years Roberto and his sister Sabrina have run this *bacaro* (hole-in-the-wall bar), serving an impressive array of local wine to a loyal group of customers who treat the place much like a social club. Join them for a glass of Raboso and heaped platters of *lardo* (cured pork fat), cheese drizzled with honey, *polpette* (meatballs) and deep-fried pumpkin. (333 3458811; Rio Terà Farsetti 1847a; meals €12, cicheti €1.50-1.80; 9am-2.30pm & 4pm-midnight Mon-Sat; San Marcuola)

Panificio Volpe Giovanni

BAKERY **€**

12  Map p100, C3

Aside from unleavened pumpkin and radicchio bread, this kosher bakery sells unusual treats such as crumbly *impade* (biscuity logs flavoured with ground almonds) and *orecchiette di Amman* (little ears of Amman; ear-shaped pastries stuffed with chocolate), along with quite possibly the best *cornetti* (Italian-style croissants) in Venice. (041 71 51 78; www.facebook.com/PanificioVolpeGiovanni; Calle Ghetto Vecchio 1143; pastries €1.50-3; 8.30am-noon Sun, 6.30am-7.30pm Mon-Fri; Guglie)

Canalside restaurants

Gelateria Ca' d'Oro

GELATO €

13 Map p100, F5

Foot traffic stops here for spectacularly creamy gelato made in-house daily. For a summer pick-me-up, try the *granita di caffe con panna* (coffee shaved ice with whipped cream). (041 522 89 82; Strada Nova 4273b; scoops €1.80; 10am-10pm; Ca' d'Oro)

Alle Due Gondolette

VENETIAN €€

14 Map p100, B2

It's worth walking the extra mile to this humble traditional eatery for its pasta and *baccalà* (cod), either creamed with olive oil, lemon and parsley or *alla Vicentina* (braised with onions, anchovies and milk). (041 71 75 23; www.alleduegondolette.com; Fondamente de le Capuzine 3016; meals €24-32; noon-2.30pm Mon-Thu, noon-2.30pm & 7-10.30pm Fri & Sat; Tre Archi)

Drinking

Il Santo Bevitore

PUB

15 Map p100, E3

San Marco has its glittering cathedral, but beer lovers prefer pilgrimages to this shrine of the 'Holy Drinker' for 20 brews on tap, including Trappist ales and seasonal stouts – alongside a big range of speciality gin, whisky and vodka. The faithful receive canalside

BEPSY/SHUTTERSTOCK ©

Casinò Di Venezia (p110)

seating, footy matches on TV, free wi-fi and the occasional live band. (335 8415771; www.ilsantobevitorepub.com; Calle Zancani 2393a; 4pm-2am; ; Ca' d'Oro)

Torrefazione Cannaregio CAFE

16 Map p100, C3

Venetians can't catch a train without a pit stop at this aromatic shopfront lined with brass-knobbed coffee bins. Since 1930, Venice's Marchi family has been importing speciality beans, roasted fresh daily in a washtub-size roaster behind the marble bar and ground to order. Service is as perky and efficient as you'd hope from such a well-caffeinated place. (041 71 63 71; www.torrefazionecannaregio.it; Rio Terà San Leonardo 1337; 7am-7.15pm; Guglie)

La Cantina WINE BAR

17 Map p100, E4

While you can sit down out the back for a serious seafood feast, we prefer to sample the wine and *cicheti* selection propped up at the bar or at one of the tables on the square fashioned from old wine barrels. (041 522 82 58; Campo San Felice 3689; 11am-11pm Mon-Sat; Ca' d'Oro)

El Sbarlefo BAR

18 Map p100, F4

All sorts sidle into this attractive little *cicheti* bar, from local hipsters to candidates for hip replacements, drawn by an excellent wine selection and a tasty array of snacks. The music meanders unpredictably from mellow jazz to early Elvis, but never at volumes to interrupt a decent chat. (☎041 523 30 84; www.elsbarlefo.it; Salizada del Pistor 4556c; ⏱10am-11pm; 📶; ⛴Ca' d'Oro)

Dodo Caffè

BAR

19 Map p100, C2

For sunsets as rosy as your *aperol spritz,* arrive early to snag canalside seating at this local favourite. The Dodo crew offer a warm welcome to strangers, along with generously stuffed *panini* and *tramezzini.* (☎041 71 59 05; www.facebook.com/DodoCaffe; Fondamenta dei Ormesini 2845; ⏱8am-2pm & 5-8.15pm; ⛴San Marcuola)

Birre da Tutto il Mondo o Quasi

BAR

20 Map p100, D2

While the rest of Venice is awash in wine, 'Beers from Around the World or Almost' offers more than 100 brews, including reasonably priced bottles of speciality craft ales and local Birra Venezia. The cheery, beery scene often spills into the street – but keep it down, or the neighbours will get testy. (☎041 71 58 34; Fondamenta dei Ormesini 2710; ⏱11am-4pm & 6pm-2am Mon-Sat; ⛴Orto)

Bagatela

BAR

21 Map p100, C2

An unpretentious, popular, late-night hang-out crammed with Cannaregio locals, indie rockers and students, Bagatela offers bottled beers, cocktails, board games, sport on the TV and a rather disconcerting skull behind the bar. Pace your alcoholic intake with one of its legendary burgers. (☎328 7255782; www.bagatelavenezia.com; Fondamente de le Capuzine 2925; ⏱6pm-1am Wed-Sun; ⛴Guglie)

Entertainment

Paradiso Perduto

LIVE MUSIC

22 Map p100, E3

'Paradise Lost' is a find for anyone craving a cold beer canalside on a hot summer's night. Although the restaurant is also popular, the Paradiso is particularly noted for its Monday night gigs; Chet Baker, Keith Richards

Local Life

Dressing for Carnevale

If you're wondering where Cinderella goes to find the perfect ball gown for Carnevale or Prince Charming his tights, look no further than **Nicolao Atelier** (☎041 520 70 51; www.nicolao.com; Fondamenta de la Misericordia 2590; ⏱9.30am-6pm Mon-Fri; ⛴San Marcuola). In his past life, Stefano Nicolao was an actor and an assistant costumier before finding his true calling as a scholar and curator of historical fashion, over 10,000 pieces of which are now stored in his vast studio. An exquisite handmade Carnevale outfit will set you back €250 to €300.

and Vinicio Capossela have all played the small stage. (041 72 05 81; Fondamenta de la Misericordia 2540; 11am-1am Thu-Mon; Orto)

Casinò Di Venezia

CASINO

23 Map p100, D4

Founded in 1638, the world's oldest casino only moved into its current palatial home in the 1950s. The building certainly wasn't lucky for composer Richard Wagner, who died here in 1883; the **Museo Wagner** (338 4164174; arwv@libero.it; admission free; by appointment) now occupies his suite. Slots open at 11am; to take on gaming tables, arrive after 3.30pm wearing your jacket and poker face. Arrive in style with a free water-taxi ride from Piazzale Roma. You must be at least 18 to enter the casino. (Ca' Vendramin Calergi; 041 529 71 11; www.casinovenezia.it; Calle Vendramin 2040; admission incl gaming token €10; 11am-2.30am; San Marcuola)

Shopping

Gianni Basso

STATIONERY

24 Map p100, H4

Gianni Basso doesn't advertise his letterpressing services: the clever calling cards crowding his studio window do the trick. Restaurant critic Gale Greene's title is framed

Understand

High Tides

Acqua alta (high water) isn't an emergency – it's a tide reaching 110cm above normal levels and normally happens four to six times a year, between November and April. *Acqua alta* may cause flooding in low-lying areas, but waters usually recede within five hours.

To see if *acqua alta* is likely, check Venice's Centro Maree 48-hour tidal forecast at www.comune.venezia.it. Alarms sound when *acqua alta* is expected to reach the city within two to four hours:

- One even tone (up to 110cm above normal): Barely warrants pauses in happy-hour conversation.
- Two rising tones (110cm to 120cm): You might need *stivali di gomma* (rubber boots).
- Three rising tones (around 130cm): Check Centro Maree online to see where *passarelle* (gangplank walkways) are in use.
- Four rising tones (140cm and up): Businesses may close early.

by a knife and fork, and Hugh Grant's moniker appears next to a surprisingly tame lion. Bring cash to commission business cards, ex libris, menus or invitations, and trust Signor Basso to deliver via post. (041 523 46 81; Calle del Fumo 5306; 9am-1pm & 2-6pm Mon-Fri, 9am-noon Sat; Fondamente Nove)

Balducci Borse

SHOES

25 Map p100, C3

Venice isn't known for its leatherwork, but there's always an exception to the rule and Franco Balducci is it. Step through the door of his Cannaregio workshop and you can smell the quality of the hand-picked Tuscan hides that he fashions on the premises into glossy shoulder bags and women's boots. (041 524 62 33; www.balducciborse.com; Rio Terà San Leonardo 1593; 9.30am-1pm & 2.30-7.30pm; San Marcuola)

Leonardo

JEWELLERY

26 Map p100, D3

This attractive shop stocks jewellery from some of the very best Murano glass artists, many of whom rarely sell outside their own showrooms. Chalcedony pendants in opal glass by Antonio Vaccari and contemporary statement necklaces by Igor Balbi are complemented by unique historical pieces, such as African murrine bead necklaces, so called as Venetian beads were widely traded throughout Africa. (Rio Terà San Leonardo 1703; 9.30am-7.30pm; San Marcuola)

Antichità al Ghetto

ANTIQUES

27  Map p100, C3

Instead of a souvenir T-shirt, how about taking home a memento of Venetian history: an ancient map of the canal, an etching of Venetian dandies daintily alighting from gondolas or an 18th-century cameo once worn by the most fashionable ladies in the Ghetto. (041 524 45 92; www.antichitaalghetto.com; Calle del Ghetto Vecchio 1133/4; 10am-noon & 2.30-7pm; Guglie)

Vittorio Costantini

GLASS

28 Map p100, H4

Kids and adults alike are thrilled at the magical, miniature insects, butterflies, shells and birds that Vittorio Costantini fashions out of glass using a lampwork technique. Some of these iridescent beetles have bodies made of 21 segments that need to be fused together with dazzling dexterity and speed. (041 522 22 65; www.vittoriocostantini.com; Calle del Fumo 5311; 9.30am-1pm & 2.15-5.30pm Mon-Fri; Fondamente Nove)

Explore

Castello

Stretching eastwards from San Marco, Castello is the city's largest neighbourhood, containing the Arsenale shipyards where Venetian craftsmen made seafaring history, alongside Gothic, Byzantine and Dalmation churches, frescoed orphanages where Vivaldi conducted and avant-garde Biennale pavilions. At the tip of Venice's tail is a pine-shaded park where Venetians go to rest, play and get away.

The Sights in a Day

Start with Castello's most compelling sites – the grand **Zanipolo church** (p116), Negroponte's rose-fringed Madonna in **Chiesa di San Francesco della Vigna** (p116) and Bellini's *Virgin Enthroned* in **Chiesa di San Zaccaria** (p117). All are within a stone's throw of San Marco.

Lunch at **Local** (p120) and then explore the vast engine of the city's seafaring might, the **Arsenale** (pictured left; p119), open between June and September for the annual Biennale di Venezia. Outside of those summer months, the nearby **Padiglione delle Navi** (p119) gives a taste of the city's maritime history. Then bunk off and wander south through the washing-strung backstreets to **Giardini Pubblici** (p116), have a cup of tea at **Serra dei Giardini** (p124), Napoleon's greenhouse, then stroll all the way to the park at the very tip of Venice's tail.

As the sun sets, make for Riva degli Schiavoni, the waterfront promenade. Take a pew at **Bar Terrazza Danieli** (p123) for evening *aperitivo* and then bar-hop to local hot spot Via Garibaldi. In the evening, choose between a concert at **La Pietà** (p126) or a romantic dinner at **Trattoria Corte Sconta** (p120).

Best of Venice

Architecture

Biennale Pavilions (p116)

Fondazione Querini Stampalia (p117)

Secrets

Chiesa di San Francesco della Vigna (p116)

Arsenale (p119)

Padiglione delle Navi (p119)

Shopping

Paolo Brandolisio (p127)

Ballarin (p127)

Kalimala (p126)

Getting There

Vaporetto Castello is encircled with *vaporetto* stops. Lines 4.1 and 4.2 stop at all of them as they loop around the perimeter of Venice; similarly 5.1 and 5.2 stop at all but Arsenale. Line 1 makes all the southern stops, linking them to the Grand Canal and the Lido. The busiest stop is San Zaccaria (also called San Marco San Zaccaria), with multiple jetties spread along Riva degli Schiavoni.

A
B
C
D
1
2
3
4
5
Campo SS Giovanni e Paolo
1 Zanipolo
Saliz S Zanipolo
29
C Bressane
Rio di San Marina
Rio di S Lio
C del Dose
Campo Santa Marina
26
17
C de la Malvasia
C Pindemonte
Campo San Lio
Reali Wellness Spa
11
Campo della Fava
C de la Malvasia
Saliz San Lio
C Mondo Novo
13
33
Fond dei Preti
C Lunga Santa Maria Formosa
37
24
C dei Orbi
Campo Santa Maria Formosa
Palazzo Grimani
7
19
6
Fondazione Querini Stampalia
C Querini
C de la Guerra
C dei Specchieri
C Fiubera
C d Selvadego
Ruga Giuffa
C di Mezzo
C d Magazen
16
Rio di San Severo
C d Corona
35
Museo delle Icone
C d Figher
C d Chiesa
CASTELLO
Gondola Service
Piazza San Marco
SAN MARCO
22
Saliz San Provolo
C dei Albanesi
C delle Rasse
20
Rio del Vin
5
Chiesa di San Zaccaria
Campo San Zaccaria
23
21
31
18
Riva degli Schiavoni
Barbaria de le Tole
36
C de le Capucine
C Zon
Rio di Santa Giustina
C dell' Ospedale
Fond Moro
Rio de la Tetta
Campo San Lorenzo
Borgoloco San Lorenzo
Rio di San Lorenzo
C d Madonna
8
Campiello dei Greci
Rio dei Greci
C del Lion
15
Saliz dei Greci
Rio de la Pietà
2
Scuola Dalmata di San Giorgio degli Schiavoni
C dei Furlani
Fond dei Furlani
C d Tedeum
C San Francesco
Chiesa di San Francesco della Vigna
3
C San Francesco
Rio di San Francesco
30
Campo S Ternità
C di Morion
Corta Nova
C dell'Olio
Rio del Scu
C Magno
34
C de l'Arco
Salizada Sant'Antonio
C Venier
Campo Bandiera e Moro
14
12
32
C del Pestrin
C d Erizzo
Cllo d Pescaria
Riva degli Schiavoni
Rio Ca' di Dio
C dei Forni
Riva Ca' di Dio
Arsenale
San Zaccaria A
San Zaccaria
San Zaccaria C/D
San Zaccaria B
Rio dei Giardinetti
Giardini Ex Reali
San Marco Giardinetti
Bacino di San Marco
Canale di San Marco
San Giorgio Maggiore
Campo San Giorgio
Isola di San Giorgio Maggiore

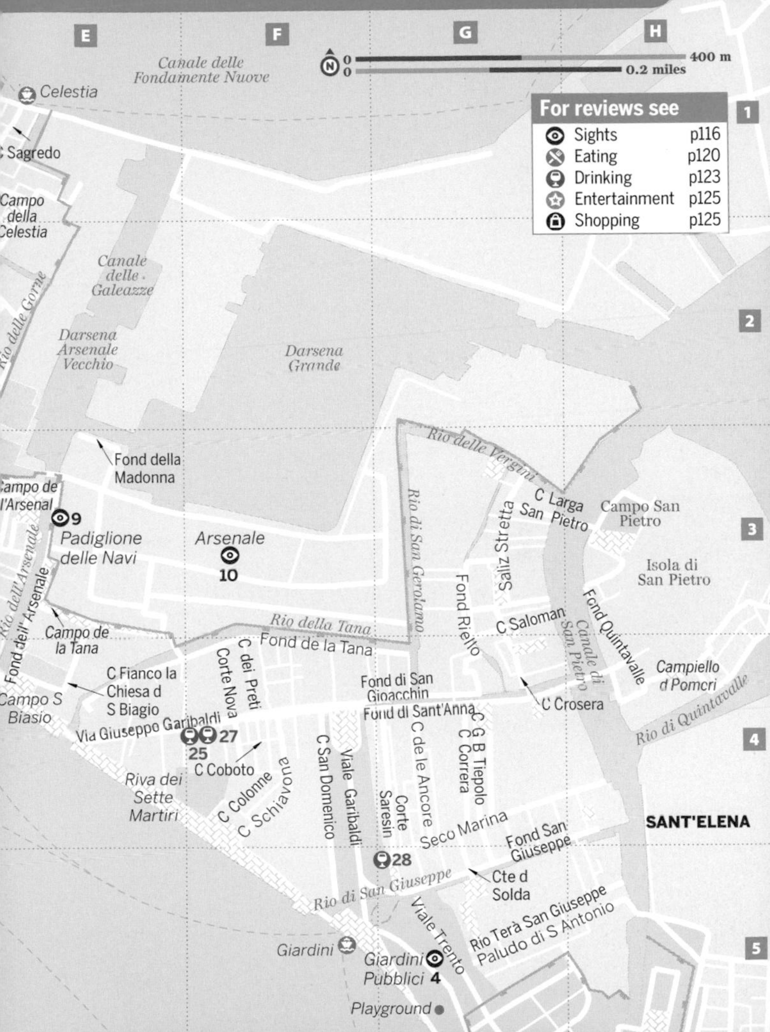

For reviews see

Sights	p116
Eating	p120
Drinking	p123
Entertainment	p125
Shopping	p125

Sights

Zanipolo
BASILICA

1 Map p114, B1

Commenced in 1333 but not finished until the 1430s, this vast church is similar in style and scope to the Franciscan Frari in San Polo which was being raised at the same time. Both oversized structures feature red-brick facades with high-contrast detailing in white stone. After its completion, Zanipolo quickly became the go-to church for ducal funerals and burials. (041 523 59 13; www.basilicasantigiovannie paolo.it; Campo Zanipolo; adult/reduced €2.50/1.25; 9am-6pm Mon-Sat, noon-6pm Sun; Ospedale)

Scuola Dalmata di San Giorgio degli Schiavoni
CHURCH

2 Map p114, C2

This 15th-century Dalmatian religious-confraternity house is dedicated to favourite Slavic saints George, Tryphon and Jerome, whose lives are captured with precision and glowing, Early Renaissance grace by 15th-century master Vittore Carpaccio. (041 522 88 28; Calle dei Furlani 3259a; adult/reduced €5/3; 1.30-5.30pm Mon, 9.30am-5.30pm Tue-Sat, 9.30am-1.30pm Sun; San Zaccaria)

Chiesa di San Francesco della Vigna
CHURCH

3 Map p114, D1

Designed and built by Jacopo Sansovino, with a facade by Palladio, this enchanting Franciscan church is one of Venice's most underappreciated attractions. The Madonna positively glows in Bellini's *Madonna and Saints* (1507) in the Cappella Santa, just off the flower-carpeted cloister, while swimming angels and strutting birds steal the scene in the delightful *Virgin Enthroned* (c 1460–70) by Antonio da Negroponte, near the door to the right of the sanctuary. Bring €0.20 to illuminate them. (Campo San Francesco 2786; admission free; 8am-12.30pm & 3-7pm; Celestia)

Giardini Pubblici
GARDENS

4 Map p114, G5

Begun under Napoleon as the city's first public green space, these leafy gardens are now the main home of the Biennale di Venezia. Only around half of the gardens is open to the public all year round as the rest is given over to the permanent **Biennale pavilions**, each representing a different country.

Local Life

Lovers' Alley

Under the arch of the covered passageway **Sotoportego dei Preti** (Arsenale) is hidden a reddish, heart-shaped stone about the size of a hand. Local lore has it that couples that touch it together will remain in love forever. Not ready to commit just yet? This is also a nice private spot for a smooch.

Madonna and Saints, Bellini, Chiesa di San Francesco della Vigna

Many of them are attractions in their own right, from Carlo Scarpa's daring 1954 raw-concrete-and-glass Venezuelan Pavilion to Denton Corker Marshall's 2015 Australian Pavilion in black granite. (Giardini)

Chiesa di San Zaccaria

CHURCH

5 Map p114, B3

When 15th-century Venetian girls showed more interest in sailors than saints, they were sent to the convent adjoining San Zaccaria. The wealth showered on the church by their grateful parents is evident. Masterpieces by Bellini, Titian, Tintoretto and Van Dyck crowd the walls. (Campo San Zaccaria 4693; admission free; 10am-noon & 4-6pm Mon-Sat, 4-6pm Sun; San Zaccaria)

Fondazione Querini Stampalia

MUSEUM

6 Map p114, B2

In 1869 Conte Giovanni Querini Stampalia made a gift of his ancestral 16th-century *palazzo* (mansion) to the city on the forward-thinking condition that its 700-year-old library operate late-night openings. Downstairs, savvy drinkers take their *aperitivi* with a twist of high modernism in the Carlo Scarpa–designed garden, while the museum's temporary exhibitions add an element of

Understand

La Biennale di Venezia

The world's most prestigious arts show is something of a misnomer: the Biennale di Venezia (www.labiennale.org) is actually held every year, but the spotlight alternates between art (odd-numbered years, eg 2017, 2019) and architecture (even-numbered years, eg 2018, 2020). The June–October art biennial presents contemporary art at 30 national pavilions in the Giardini Pubblici (p116), with additional exhibitions in venues across town. The architecture biennial is usually held September to November, filling vast Arsenale boat sheds with high-concept structures.

The History of the Biennale

Venice held its first Biennale in 1895 to reassert its role as global tastemaker and provide an essential corrective to the brutality of the Industrial Revolution. At first the Biennale retained strict control, removing a provocative Picasso from the Spanish Pavilion in 1910, but after WWII, national pavilions asserted their autonomy and the Biennale became an international avant-garde showcase.

The Pavilions

The Biennale's 29 pavilions tell a fascinating story of 20th-century architecture reflecting national identities from Hungary (futuristic folklore hut) to Canada (ski-lodge cathedral). The most recent addition is the 2015 Australian Pavilion by starchitects Denton Corker Marshall. A black granite box hidden intriguingly amid the foliage, it speaks of the imposition of European settlements on indigenous Australian lands.

Beyond the Biennale

The city-backed Biennale organisation also runs the Venice International Film Festival each September and organises an International Festival of Contemporary Dance and concert series every summer. For upcoming event listings check the website. To defray substantial costs to the city, there's an entry fee to the main art and architecture shows and film festival premieres – but many ancillary arts programs are free. When the art biennale's in town, book two months ahead for accommodation, and at least a week ahead at popular Castello restaurants.

the unexpected to the silk-draped salons upstairs. (☎041 271 14 11; www.querinistampalia.it; Campiello Querini Stampalia 5252; adult/reduced €4/2; ⏱10am-6pm Tue-Sun; ⛴San Zaccaria)

Palazzo Grimani MUSEUM

7 Map p114, B2

The Grimani family built their Renaissance *palazzo* in 1568 to showcase their extraordinary Graeco-Roman collection, which was destined to become the basis of the archaeological museum now housed in the Museo Correr (p36). Unusually for Venice, the palace has a Roman-style courtyard, which shed a flattering light on the archaeological curiosities. These days, the halls are mainly empty, though their bedazzling frescoed interiors are reason enough to visit. (☎041 520 03 45; www.palazzogrimani.org; Ramo Grimani 4858; adult/reduced €5/2.50; ⏱8.15am-7pm Tue-Sat, 2-7pm Sun; ⛴San Zaccaria)

Museo delle Icone MUSEUM

8 Map p114, C2

Glowing colours and all-seeing eyes fill this treasure box of some 80 Byzantine-style icons made in 14th- to 17th-century Italy. Keep your own eye out for the expressive *San Giovanni Climaco,* which shows the saintly author of a Greek spiritual guide distracted from his work by visions of souls diving into hell. (Museum of Icons; ☎041 522 65 81; www.istitutoellenico.org; Campo dei Greci 3412; adult/reduced €4/2; ⏱9am-5pm; ⛴San Zaccaria)

Padiglione delle Navi MUSEUM

9 Map p114, E3

An annexe of the **Museo Storico Navale** (closed at the time of research for renovations), the Padiglione delle Navi is a vast 2000-sq-metre warehouse containing a fabulous collection of historic boats, including typical Venetian luggers, gondolas, racing boats, military vessels, a funerary barge and a royal motorboat. (Ships Pavilion; ☎041 24 24; www.visitmuve.it; Fondamenta de la Madonna 2162c; adult/reduced €5/3.50; ⏱2pm & 3.30pm Sat, 11am, 12.30pm, 2pm & 3.30pm Sun; ⛴Arsenale)

Arsenale HISTORIC SITE

10 Map p114, F3

Founded in 1104, the Arsenale soon became the greatest medieval shipyard in Europe, home to 300 shipping companies employing up to 16,000 people. Capable of turning out a new galley in a day, it is considered a forerunner of mass industrial production. Though it's closed to the public most of the year, arty types invade the shipyard during Venice's art and architecture Biennales, when it hosts exhibitions and special events. (http://arsenale.comune.venezia.it; ⛴Arsenale)

Reali Wellness Spa

SPA

11 Map p114, A2

In this surprisingly spa-starved city, the Hotel ai Reali's spa offers a sanctuary of Asian-inspired wellness. Instead of being banished to the basement as is usually the case, the Reali's spa is on the top floor where light floods into the Turkish bath and soothes you in your 'emotional' shower. A range of Thai massages and beauty treatments is offered. (041 241 59 16; www.hotelaireali.com; Campo de la Fava 5527; 4hr sessions €25; 10am-9pm; Rialto)

Eating

Trattoria Corte Sconta

VENETIAN **€€€**

12 Map p114, D3

Well-informed visitors and celebrating locals seek out this vine-covered *corte sconta* (hidden courtyard) for its trademark seafood antipasti and imaginative house-made pasta. Inventive flavour pairings transform the classics: clams zing with ginger; prawn and courgette linguine is recast with an earthy dash of saffron; and the roast eel loops like the Brenta River in a drizzle of balsamic reduction. (041 522 70 24; www.cortescontavenezia.it; Calle del Pestrin 3886; meals €44-53; 12.30-2pm & 7-9.30pm Tue-Sat, closed Jan & Aug; ; Arsenale)

Alle Testiere

VENETIAN **€€€**

13 Map p114, A2

Make a reservation for one of the two evening sittings at this tiny restaurant and come prepared for one of Bruno Gavagnin's beautifully plated seafood feasts. Subtle spices such as ginger, cinnamon and orange zest recall Venice's trading past with the East. (041 522 72 20; www.osterialletestiere.it; Calle del Mondo Novo 5801; meals €49-57; 12.30-3pm & 7-11pm Tue-Sat; Rialto)

CoVino

VENETIAN **€€**

14 Map p114, D3

Tiny CoVino has only 14 seats but demonstrates bags of ambition in its inventive, seasonal menu inspired by the Venetian terroir. Speciality products are selected from Slow Food Presidio producers, and the charming waiters make enthusiastic recommendations from the interesting wine list. Only the set menu is available at dinner, but there's an à la carte selection at lunch. (041 241 27 05; www.covinovenezia.com; Calle del Pestrin 3829; 3-course menu €39; 12.30-3.30pm & 7pm-1am Thu-Mon; ; Arsenale)

Local

VENETIAN **€€€**

15 Map p114, C2

Although he's cooked in fine-dining establishments like Locanda Locatelli, Noma and the Cipriani, chef Matteo Tagliapietra grew up on the

MASSIMILIANO DONATI/SHUTTERSTOCK ©

One of the Biennale pavilions in the Giardini Pubblici (p116)

fisherman's island of Burano. As such his simple, seasonal cooking is rooted in the lagoon and his dishes, while creative, remain honest and flavourful. Highlights of the ever-changing menu include humble Gò risotto and the chocolate *barene* (sandbank) dessert. (☎041 241 11 28; www.ristorantelocal.com; Salizada dei Greci 3303; meals €75; ⏰noon-2pm & 7-10pm Thu-Mon, 7-10pm Wed; ❄; ⛴San Zaccaria)

Al Giardinetto da Severino VENETIAN €€

16 Map p114, B2

Date nights don't come better than sitting among a sea of greenery in Al Giardinetto's vine-covered courtyard. For nearly 70 years the Bastianello-Parmesan family have run this restaurant in the former chapel of the 15th-century Palazzo Zorzi. In that time they've perfected traditional dishes such as crab pasta, bean soup and veal schnitzel. (☎041 528 53 32; www.algiardinetto.it; Salizada Zorzi 4928; meals €34-44; ⏰noon-3pm & 7-10pm Fri-Wed, closed Jan; ⛴San Zaccaria)

Didovich BAKERY, DELI €

17 Map p114, A1

With outside seating on pretty Campo Santa Marina, cheerful Didovich offers the rare opportunity to sit down for a cooked breakfast. Otherwise, join the locals propping up the counter, sipping coffee and munching on croissants and *fritelle* (doughnuts). At lunchtime, sweets change to savouries with an option to take out portions of homemade pasta dishes or *polpette* (meatballs). (041 523 00 17; Campo Santa Marina 5908; pastries €1.10, mains €8-10; 7am-8pm Mon-Sat; Rialto)

Wildner

VENETIAN €€€

18 Map p114, C3

Occupying a glass pavilion jutting out onto the Riva, Pensione Wildner's longstanding restaurant serves delicious takes on traditional Venetian dishes, such as octopus on lentils and veal liver on polenta. The prime waterfront position means that the prices are perhaps higher than they should be, but the lunch special (two courses and wine for €20) is an absolute steal. (041 522 74 63; www.hotelwildner.com; Riva degli Schiavoni 4161; meals €44-55; noon-10pm Wed-Mon; San Zaccaria)

Local Life

Venice Music Gourmet

Hosted in historic palaces, these **gourmet musical evenings** (391 3592959; www.venicemusicgourmet.it; dinner, drinks & concert €110; 7pm Thu & Fri; San Zaccaria, Celestia) promise stirring tunes from Vivaldi and Bach, as well as Italian jazz legends, accompanied by a multi-course dinner of lagoon delights. It's exactly how Venetians past would have heard the latest tracks amid a convivial group of guests knocking back first-class glasses of Franciacorta and forkfuls of *sarde in saor* (grilled sardines in a sweet and sour sauce).

Osteria Ruga di Jaffa

OSTERIA €€

19 Map p114, B2

Hiding in plain sight on the busy Ruga Giuffa is this *osteria* (casual tavern) with artsy Murano wall lamps. You should be able to spot it by the gondoliers packing out the tables at lunchtime; they come to feast on the massive serves of pasta and delicious homemade bread. Be warned: there's no English menu. (041 241 10 62; www.osteriarugadijaffa.it; Ruga Giuffa 4864; meals €29-41; 7am-11pm; San Zaccaria)

Trattoria alla Rivetta

VENETIAN €€

20 Map p114, B3

Tucked behind the Ponte San Provolo, this trattoria hums with the chatter of contented diners even in the dead of winter. It is staffed by a clutch of senior waiters in jovial red waistcoats, who'll cordially serve you platters of lagoon fare such as raw seafood antipasti, pasta with clams and *fritto misto* (mixed fried seafood). (041 528 73 02; Salizada San Provolo 4625; meals €26-42; 10am-10.30pm Tue-Sun; San Zaccaria)

Drinking

Bar Dandolo

COCKTAIL BAR

21 Map p114, B3

Dress to the nines and swan straight past the 'hotel guests only' sign to the glamorous bar filling the grand hall of the 14th-century Palazzo Dandolo. Sparkles from Murano chandeliers reflect off the gilt edges and silk furnishings, while snappily dressed staff effortlessly descend with signature Vesper martinis and tasty, bottomless bowls of snacks. (041 522 64 80; www.danielihotelvenice.com; Riva degli Schiavoni 4196; 9.30am-1.15am; San Zaccaria)

Bacaro Risorto

BAR

22  Map p114, B3

Just a footbridge from San Marco, this shoebox of a corner bar overflowing with happy drinkers offers quality wines and abundant *cicheti* (Venetian tapas), including *crostini* (open-faced sandwiches) heaped with *sarde in saor*, soft cheeses and melon tightly swaddled in prosciutto. Note that opening times are 'flexible'. (Campo San Provolo 4700; 8am-1am; San Zaccaria)

Bar Terrazza Danieli

BAR

23 Map p114, B3

Gondolas glide in to dock along the quay, while across the lagoon the white-marble edifice of Palladio's San Giorgio Maggiore turns from gold to pink in the waters of the canal: the late-afternoon scene from the Hotel Danieli's top-floor balcony bar definitely calls for a toast. Linger over a *spritz* or cocktail. (041 522 64 80; www.danielihotelvenice.com; Riva degli Schiavoni 4196; 3-7pm May-Sep; San Zaccaria)

Enoteca Mascareta

WINE BAR

24 Map p114, B1

Oenophiles love this traditional *enoteca* (wine bar) for its stellar wines by the glass, including big Amarones and organic 'cloudy' *prosecco*, one of them made by owner Mauro. If you're hungry, the excellent *taier misto* (platters of cured meats and cheeses) could pass for a light meal for two. (041 523 07 44; Calle Lunga Santa Maria Formosa 5183; 7pm-2am Fri-Tue; Ospedale)

Strani

BAR

25 Map p114, F4

There's always a party on at Strani thanks to its excellent selection of beers on tap, well-priced glasses of Veneto wines and platters of *sopressa* (soft salami). A plethora of *cicheti* keeps drinkers fuelled for late-night jam sessions with the locals. (041 099 14 34; www.straninvenice.it; Via Garibaldi 1582; 7.30am-1am summer, noon-10pm winter; Giardini)

Rosa Salva

Al Portego

BAR

26 Map p114, A1

This walk-in closet somehow manages to distribute wine, craft beer and *cicheti* to the overflowing crowd of young Venetians in approximate order of arrival. Wine is cheap and plentiful, and the bar groans with classic nibbles. If that's not enough, make a dash for one of the five tables around the back where enormous plates of seafood are served. (041 522 90 38; Corte Spechiera 6014; 11am-3pm & 5.30-10pm; Rialto)

El Rèfolo

BAR

27 Map p114, F4

Although the bars along Via Garibaldi may look interchangeable, the queue for El Rèfolo's pavement tables says otherwise. Part of the draw is the ever-friendly Massimiliano dispensing Italian microbrews and glasses of wine, as well as the plump sandwiches and summertime live music. (Via Garibaldi 1580; noon-12.30am Tue-Sun; Giardini)

Serra dei Giardini

CAFE

28 Map p114, G5

This attractive iron-framed greenhouse was built in 1894 to house the palms used in Biennale events.

It rapidly expanded into a social hub and a centre for propagation: many plants grown here adorned the municipal flowerbeds of the Lido and the ballrooms of aristocratic *palazzi* (mansions). Restored in 2010, it now has a cafe and hosts events, exhibitions and workshops. (041 296 03 60; www.serradeigiardini.org; Viale Garibaldi 1254; admission free; 10am-8pm; Giardini)

Rosa Salva

CAFE

29 Map p114, B1

For over a century, Rosa Salva has been serving tea, pastries and ice creams to the passing trade on Campo Zanipolo. Inside the 1930s throwback interior, ladies take *tramezzini* (triangular, stacked sandwiches) and trays of *tè con limone* at marble-topped tables while, outside, sunseekers sip *spritz* and children slurp ice creams. (041 522 79 49; www.rosasalva.it; Campo Zanipolo 6779; 8am-8pm; Ospedale)

Entertainment

Laboratorio Occupato Morion

LIVE MUSIC

30 Map p114, D2

When not busy staging environmental protests or avant-garde performance art, this counterculture social centre throws one hell of a party, with performances by bands from around the Veneto. Events are announced via posters thrown up around town and on its Facebook page. (www.facebook.com/laboratorioccupatomorion; Salizada San Francesco 2951; Celestia)

Collegium Ducale

CLASSICAL MUSIC

31 Map p114, B3

Spend a perfectly enjoyable evening in prison with this six-member chamber orchestra, who perform Vivaldi's *Four Seasons* in the grand hall rather than the cells. On alternate nights opera singers tackle everything from Mozart to Gerswhin accompanied only by a piano. (041 98 42 52; www.collegiumducale.com; Palazzo delle Prigioni 4209; tickets €28; San Zaccaria)

Shopping

Atelier Alessandro Merlin

HOMEWARES

32 Map p114, D3

Enjoy your breakfast in the nude, on a horse or atop a jellyfish – Alessandro Merlin paints them all on striking black and white cappuccino cups and saucers. Homoerotic-art lovers will recognise the influence of Tom of Finland in his ultra-masculine, well-endowed, nude dudes, but the *sgraffito* technique he uses on some of his work dates back to Roman times. (041 522 58 95; Calle del Pestrin 3876; 10am-noon & 3-7pm Mon-Thu & Sat, 3-7pm Fri & Sun; Arsenale)

Understand

Vivaldi's Orphan Orchestra

Over the centuries, Venetian musicians developed a reputation for playing music as though their lives depended on it – which at times wasn't far from the truth. With shrinking 17th-century trade revenues, the state took the quixotic step of underwriting musical education for orphan girls, and the investment yielded surprising returns.

Among the maestri hired to conduct orphan-girl orchestras was Antonio Vivaldi (1678–1741), whose 30-year tenure yielded hundreds of concertos and popularised Venetian baroque music across Europe. Visitors spread word of extraordinary performances by orphan girls, and the city became a magnet for novelty-seeking, moneyed socialites.

Modern visitors to Venice can still see music and opera performed in the same venues as in Vivaldi's day – including Tiepolo-frescoed **La Pietà** (041 522 21 71; www.pietavenezia.org; Riva degli Schiavoni; €3, guided tours €10; 9am-5pm Sat & Sun, tours noon Tue-Fri; San Zaccaria), the *ospedaletto* (orphanage) where Vivaldi was the musical director.

Kalimala SHOES

33 Map p114, A2

Sleek belts with brushed-steel buckles, satchels, man-bags and knee-high red boots: Kalimala makes beautiful leather goods in practical, modern styles. Shoes, sandals and gloves are crafted from vegetable-cured cow hide and dyed in a mix of earthy tones and vibrant lapis blues. Given the natural tanning and top-flight leather, the prices are remarkably reasonable, with handmade shoes starting at €135. (041 528 35 96; www.kalimala.it; Salizada San Lio 5387; 9.30am-7.30pm Mon-Sat; Rialto)

Bragorà FASHION & ACCESSORIES

34 Map p114, D2

Bragorà is a multipurpose space: part shop, service centre and cultural hub. Its upcycled products include beach bags sewn out of boat sails, toy gondolas fashioned from drink cans, belts made from bike tyres and jewellery crafted from springs. There's an excellent range of witty tees on Venetian themes and you can even print your own. (041 319 08 64; www.bragora.it; Salizada Sant'Antonin 3496; 9.30am-7.30pm; Arsenale)

Paolo Brandolisio

ARTS & CRAFTS

35 Map p114, B2

Beneath all the marble and gilt, Venice is a city of wood long supported by its carpenters, caulkers, oarmakers and gilders. Master woodcarver Paolo Brandolisio continues the traditions, crafting the sinuous *forcola* (rowlock) that supports the gondolier's oar. Made of walnut or cherry wood, each is crafted specifically for boat and gondolier. Miniature replicas are on sale in the workroom. (041 522 41 55; Sotoportego Corte Rota 4725; 9am-1pm & 3-7pm Mon-Fri; San Zaccaria)

Qshop

BOOKS, HOMEWARES

Aside from its sumptuous range of art and design books, the shop of the Fondazione Querini Stampalia (see 6 Map114, B2) offers a highly curated selection of glass, jewellery, household items, silverware and textiles. Pieces from design greats such as Carlo Scarpa, Carlo Moretti and San Lorenzo sit beside the work of emerging talents. (041 523 44 11; www.querinistampalia.it; Campiello Querini Stampalia 5252; 10am-6pm Tue-Sun; San Zaccaria)

Ballarin

ANTIQUES

36 Map p114, C1

If you're looking for something distinctively Venetian, check out this Aladdin's cave. An old-fashioned dealer and artisan restorer, Valter Ballarin has a knack for tracking down period furnishings, hand-painted glassware, prints, books, toys and lamps. The best souvenir, though, is a handful of colourful, hand-blown glass flowers from dismembered Murano chandeliers. (347 7792492; Calle del Cafetier 6482; 10am-1pm & 4-6.30pm Mon-Sat; Ospedale)

Al Campanil

JEWELLERY

37 Map p114, B1

Utilising traditional Murano techniques and materials, including oxides and resins, Sabina Melinato conjures up gleaming contemporary glass and costume jewellery. Her deco-inspired glass pendants are so highly polished they look like lacquerwork – just what you'd expect from a teacher at Murano's International School of Glass. (041 523 57 34; Calle Lunga Santa Maria Formosa 5184; 9.30am-12.30pm & 3.30-7.30pm Mon-Sat; Ospedale)

Explore

The Lagoon & the Islands

Other cities have suburban sprawl and malls; Venice has a teal-blue lagoon dotted with photogenic islands and rare wildlife. Outlying islands range from celebrated glass centres and former Byzantine capitals to beach resorts and arty isles, sometimes divided only by a narrow channel.

The Sights in a Day

Plan your trip carefully around your priorities – or it can be tricky to squeeze in Murano glass, Burano photography and Torcello mosaics. Hit the **Basilica di Santa Maria Assunta** (p132) on Torcello first. From the *campanile* (bell tower) you get a fantastic view over the lagoon, after which you can segue into a leisurely lunch at **Locanda Cipriani** (p143).

Alternatively, skip over to tiny Mazzorbo and lunch at contemporary bistro **Venissa** (p144), then stroll around the multicoloured fishermen's houses on Burano (pictured left) before heading back to Murano for an art-glass blitz. Before buying, check out the exhibits at the **Museo del Vetro** (p135).

As *aperitivo* hour beckons, head for the southern island of Giudecca to catch the sun striking the peerless Palladio facade of **Basilica di San Giorgio Maggiore** (p130). Then toast the day's adventures at **La Palanca** (p143) before settling down for a memorable dinner at **Trattoria Altanella** (p143).

For a local's day on the Lagoon & the Islands, see p134, p136 and p138.

Top Sights

Local Life

Best of Venice

Secrets

Getting There

Vaporetto Giudecca: lines 2, 4.1, 4.2 and N (night) from San Marco or Dorsoduro; San Giorgio Maggiore: line 2 from San Zaccaria; Lido: lines 1, 2, 5.1, 5.2, 6, 8, 10 and 14; Murano: lines 3, 4.1 or 4.2, lines 12 and 13 stop only at Faro; Burano, Mazzorbo and Torcello: line 12 from Fondamente Nove or Murano-Faro stop; line 9 from Burano also heads to Torcello; Le Vignole and Sant'Erasmo: line 13 from Fondamente Nove via Murano-Faro.

Top Sights
Basilica di San Giorgio Maggiore

Solar eclipses are only marginally more dazzling than the view of this abbey church (completed 1610), positioned for maximum impact on its own island facing San Marco. Palladio chose white Istrian stone to stand out against the blue lagoon waters, and set it at an angle to create visual drama while also ensuring that it catches the sun all afternoon.

Map p140, C3

041 522 78 27

www.abbaziasangiorgio.it

Isola di San Giorgio Maggiore

bell tower adult/reduced €6/4

8.30am-6pm

San Giorgio Maggiore

Palladio's Facade

Palladio's radical facade gracefully solved the problem bedevilling Renaissance church design: how to graft a triangular, classical pediment onto a Christian church, with its high, central nave and lower side aisles. Palladio's solution: use one pediment to crown the nave, and a lower, half-pediment to span both side aisles. The two interlock with rhythmic harmony, while prominent three-quarter columns, deeply incised capitals and sculptural niches create depth with clever shadow-play. Above the facade rises a brick *campanile* with a conical copper spire and a cap of Istrian stone.

Interior

Likewise, the interior is an uncanny combination of brightness and serenity. Sunlight enters through high thermal windows and is then diffused by acres of white stucco. Floors inlaid with white, red and black stone draw the eye toward the altar. With its rigorous application of classical motifs, it's reminiscent of a Roman theatre.

Tintorettos

Two outstanding late works by Tintoretto flank the church's altar. On one side hangs his *Collection of Manna;* on the other side, *Last Supper* depicts Christ and his apostles in a scene that looks suspiciously like a 16th-century Venetian tavern, with a cat and dog angling for scraps. Nearby hangs what is considered to be Tintoretto's final masterpiece, the moving *Deposition of Christ.*

☑ Top Tips

▶ Take the lift to the top of the bell tower, where you can catch a unique view back across the lagoon – it's cheaper than San Marco's *campanile* and you won't have to queue.

▶ Tintoretto's final work, the moving *Deposition of Christ,* hangs within the Cappella dei Morti, which is accessed from the sanctuary but only open for Mass.

Take a Break

There's nowhere to eat on the island itself so jump on the number 2 *vaporetto* to Giudecca for a quick bite at La Palanca (p143).

For a more upmarket meal, try Trattoria Altanella (p143).

Top Sights
Basilica di Santa Maria Assunta & Torcello

Life choices are presented in no uncertain terms in Santa Maria Assunta's vivid cautionary tale: look ahead to a golden afterlife amid saints and a beatific Madonna, or turn your back on her to face the wrath of a devil gloating over lost souls. In existence since the 7th century, this former cathedral is the lagoon's oldest Byzantine-Romanesque structure.

Map p140, E1

041 73 01 19

Piazza Torcello, Torcello

adult/reduced €5/4, incl museum €8/6, incl audio guide & campanile €12/10

10am-5pm

Torcello

Detail, *Last Judgement* mosaic

Madonna & Last Judgment Mosaics

The restrained brick exterior betrays no hint of the colourful scene that unfolds as you enter. The Madonna rises in the east like the sun above a field of Torcello poppies in the 12th-century **apse mosaic**, while the back wall vividly depicts the dire consequences of dodging biblical commandments. This extraordinary **Last Judgment mosaic** shows the Adriatic as a sea nymph ushering souls lost at sea towards St Peter, while a sneaky devil tips the scales of justice and the Antichrist's minions drag sinners into hell.

Chapel Mosaics & Other Key Works

The right-hand chapel is capped with another 12th-century mosaic showing Christ flanked by angels and Sts Augustine, Ambrose, Martin and Gregory amid symbolic plants: lilies (representing purity), wheat and grapes (representing the bread and wine of the Eucharist), and poppies (evoking Torcello's island setting).

The polychrome marble floor is another medieval masterpiece, with swirling designs and interlocking wheels symbolising eternal life. Saints line up atop the gilded **iconostasis**, their gravity foiled by a Byzantine screen teeming with peacocks, rabbits and other fanciful beasts.

Museo di Torcello

Relics of Torcello's 7th- to 11th-century Byzantine empire are shown inside 13th-century Palazzo del Consiglio, home to the **Museo di Torcello** (www.museoditorcello.provincia.venezia.it; adult/reduced €3/1.50, incl basilica €8/6; ⏲10.30am-5.30pm). Exquisite mosaic fragments here show glass mastery achieved in Torcello before Murano entered the business, while upstairs archives contain Graeco-Roman artefacts from the lost civilisation of Altinum.

☑ Top Tips

- Climb the *campanile* (€5) at the rear for heavenly views over the swampy islands, giving a fascinating insight into what Venice itself must once have looked like.
- An audio guide (€2) gives further details of the church and its artworks.
- Various combo tickets are offered including the church, *campanile*, audio guide and the neighbouring museum.

Take a Break

Locanda Cipriani (p143) offers bellinis and duck pasta in a splendid rose garden. Otherwise, hop the *vaporetto* to Mazzorbo for lagoon-inspired fare in the vineyard of Venissa Osteria (p144).

Local Life
Murano Art Glass

Unrivalled masters of art glass since the 10th century, Venice's glass artisans moved to Murano in the 13th century to contain *fornace* (furnace) fire hazards. Trade secrets were so jealously guarded that glass masters who left the city were threatened with assassination. Today, Murano glass masters ply their trade along Fondamenta dei Vetrai and Ramo di Mula, and their wares are unmatched.

1 Basilica, Bones & Mosaics

In medieval **Basilica dei SS Maria e Donato** (www.sandonatomurano.it; Campo San Donato; admission free; 9am-6pm Mon-Sat, 12.30-6pm Sun; Museo) a 12th-century gilded-glass mosaic Madonna made in Murano's *fornaci* graces the apse and the bones of a dragon hang behind the altar – according to legend, slayed by St Donatus of Arezzo, whose remains also rest here. Underfoot is a 12th-century mosaic floor.

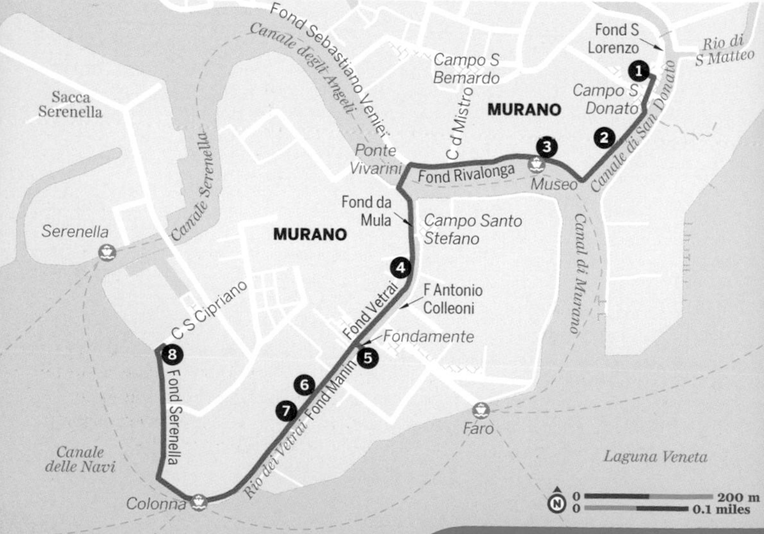

❷ Glass Museum

Since 1861, Murano's glass-making prowess has been celebrated at the **Museo del Vetro** (Glass Museum; ☎041 527 47 18; www.museovetro.visitmuve.it; Fondamenta Giustinian 8; adult/reduced €10/7.50, free with Museum Pass; ⏰10am-5pm; ⛴Museo) in Palazzo Giustinian, and renovations finally do justice to the fabulous collection. On entry a video geeks out on the technical processes, while upstairs eight rooms have beautifully curated displays of objects dating back to the 5th century BC.

❸ Davide Penso Beadwork

Davide Penso (☎041 527 56 59; www.davidepenso.com; Fondamenta Rivalonga 48; ⏰10am-6pm Mon-Sat; ⛴Museo) has taken the art of bead-making global, with African-inspired necklaces exhibited at Boston's Fine Arts Museum. Lamp-worked beads in essential shapes are strung onto modern necklaces and bracelets that look ancient.

❹ Necklace DIY

Salvadore (Map p140, C2; ☎041 73 67 72; Fondamenta dei Vetrai 128a; ⏰10.30am-6pm Mon-Sat; ⛴Colonna) specialises in light-hearted creations: aqua and yellow bead necklaces look like strands of tiny beach balls. Aspiring designers can create their own looks from individual blown-glass beads (€3 to €15 per bead).

❺ Cutting Edge at ElleElle

Nason Moretti has made modernist magic in glass since the 1950s, and at **ElleElle** (☎041 527 48 66; www.elleellemurano.com; Fondamenta Manin 52; ⏰10.30am-1pm & 2-6pm; ⛴Faro) is breaking ground with collections for New York's MoMA. Prices start at €30 for signed, blown-glass drinking glasses.

❻ Modern Classics at Venini

Of the big houses, **Venini** (☎041 273 72 04; www.venini.it; Fondamenta dei Vetrai 47; ⏰9.30am-6pm Mon-Sat; ⛴Colonna) remains the most relevant, defining modernist trends since the 1930s. Collaborations feature design greats like Carlo Scarpa and Fabio Novembre, who created giant glass 'Happy Pills' for Venini.

❼ Winged Goblets at Toffolo

Classic gold-leafed winged goblets and mind-boggling miniatures are the legendary master glass-blower's trademarks at **Cesare Toffolo** (☎041 73 64 60; www.toffolo.com; Fondamenta dei Vetrai 37; ⏰10am-6pm; ⛴Colonna), but you'll also find some dramatic departures: striking jet-black vases and light-as-air drinking glasses.

❽ Sent Studio Jewels

The Sent sisters are fourth-generation glassmakers, and their new light-filled, exposed-concrete **Marina e Susanna Sent Studio** (☎041 527 46 65; www.marinaesusannasent.com; Fondamenta Serenella 20; ⏰10am-5pm Mon-Fri; ⛴Colonna) is as strikingly modern as their jewellery: ice-blue glass waterfall necklaces, lava-red beads on paper collars. Ask to open jewellery drawers to browse hidden treasures.

Local Life
Getting Creative in Giudecca

Once the glamorous garden-villa island getaway of Venice's elite, Giudecca became a military-industrial complex in the 19th century. Now its brutalist factories, barracks and arsenals are being creatively repurposed into industrial-cool hubs by Venice's creative class. Whether your creative aspirations are in design, art, cuisine, theatre, architecture, music or photography, Giudecca is an island of inspiration.

1 Design Schemes at Fortuny

Find out why Marcel Proust waxed rhapsodic over Fortuny's silken cottons printed with art nouveau patterns at **Fortuny Tessuti Artistici** (393 8257651; www.fortuny.com; Fondamenta San Biagio 805; 10am-6pm Mon-Fri; Palanca). Dream up decor ideas browsing some 300 textile designs, but don't expect to find out how it's done – fabrication methods have

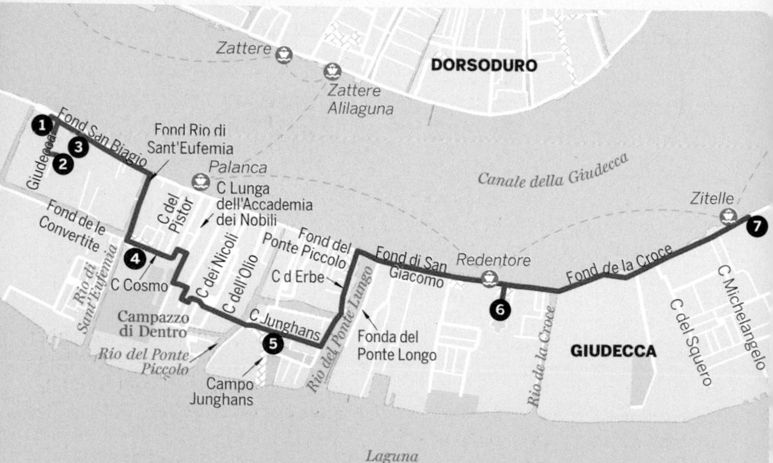

been jealously guarded in the garden studio for a century.

2 Brewery Events Space

Non-profit gallery **Spazio Punch** (www.spaziopunch.com) have transformed Giudecca's derelict beer factory into an occasional venue for temporary art, design and fashion events, which take place several times a year.

3 Emerging Art at Giudecca 795

Kickstart art collections with original works by emerging local artists at **Giudecca 795** (☎340 8798327; www.giudecca795.com; Fondamenta San Biagio 795; admission free; 🕘6-9pm Tue-Fri & Sun, 3.30-8pm Sat; ⛴Palanca) – before they get discovered at the Biennale di Venezia.

4 Holy Artisans!

The cloister of the former Convent of Sts Cosmas and Damian has been repurposed as **Artigiani del Chiostro** (Campo San Cosma; 🕘hours vary; ⛴Palanca), a base for independent artisans to ply their craft. Each keeps their own hours and not all are open to the public, but loop around and you'll find traditional mask makers, antique restorers, artists, metal workers, glass-blowers and many, many cats.

5 Arsenal Theatrics

Make art, not war at this modern theatre built on the site of a former arsenal. **Teatro Junghans** (☎041 241 19 74; www.accademiateatraleveneta.com; Campo Junghans 494; prices vary; 👪; ⛴Redentore) stages original works and offers workshops on costume design and *commedia dell'arte* (traditional masked theatre) – check the online calendar for performances.

6 Triumph at Il Rendentore

Palladio's 1577–92 **Il Redentore** (Church of the Most Holy Redeemer; www.chorusvenezia.org; Campo del SS Redentore 194; adult/reduced €3/1.50, with Chorus Pass free; 🕘10.30am-4.30pm Mon-Sat; ⛴Redentore) is a triumph of white marble celebrating the city's deliverance from the Black Death. Inside above the portal, Paolo Piazza's strikingly modern 1619 *Gratitude of Venice for Liberation* from the Plague shows the city held aloft by angels in sobering shades of grey.

7 Photography at Tre Oci

The view of San Marco from the three porthole windows at **Casa dei Tre Oci** (☎041 241 23 32; www.treoci.org; Fondamente de le Zitelle 43; adult/reduced €12/10; 🕘10am-6pm Wed-Mon; ⛴Zitelle) may inspire your own photographic masterpieces, as may the shows of contemporary photography and art held here. Once the home of early 20th-century artist and photographer Mario de Maria, this neo-Gothic landmark is now a cultural centre run by Fondazione di Venezia.

Local Life
Beaches & Bars on the Lido

Beach chairs and bronzed life-guards may seem a world apart from muggy central Venice in summer, but they're only a 15-minute ferry ride away. Sandy beaches line the seaward side of the Lido; they're packed in summer although their gentle gradient makes them perfect for toddlers but a little frustrating for adults. For adults, there's refreshing cocktails and epic summer-weekend DJ sessions and beach concerts.

1 Beach-Hop by Bicycle

To tour at your own pace, rent a set of wheels from friendly **Lido on Bike** (041 526 80 19; www.lidoonbike.it; Gran Viale Santa Maria Elisabetta 21b; bicycle rental per 90min/day €5/9; 9am-7pm summer; Lido SME). Reasonable prices include a free map with recommended routes. Identification showing you're at least 18 is required.

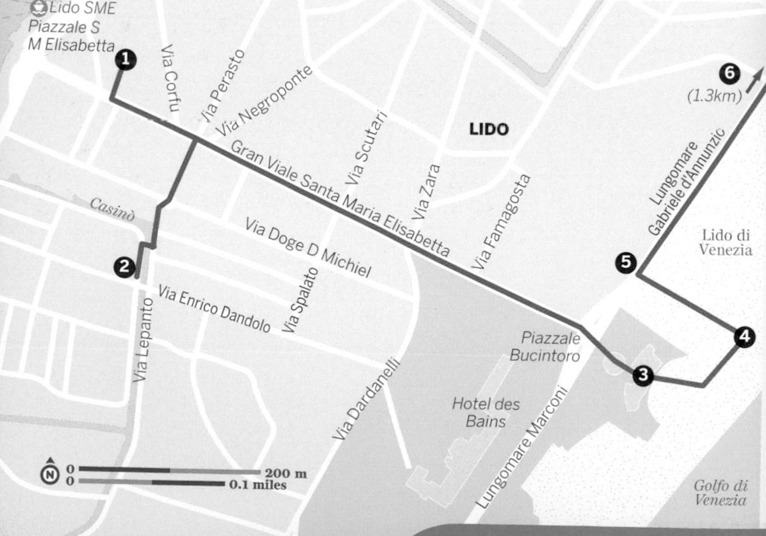

2 Drink Like a Fish at al Mercà

Located in the old Lido fish market, **al Mercà** (☎041 243 16 63; www.osteriaalmerca.it; Via Enrico Dandolo 17a; meals €28-40, set lunch 2-/3-courses €15/20; ⊙10.30am-3pm & 6.15-11pm Tue-Sun; Lido SME) is a year-round draw for its abundant *cicheti* (Venetian tapas), outdoor seating and well-priced wine by the glass. Take a pew at one of the marble counters and order up a seafood storm of *folpetti* (mini octopus), fried *schìe* (shrimp) and creamy salt cod.

3 Summer Events at Blue Moon

From afar, the domed semicircular structure of **Blue Moon** (Piazzale Bucintoro 1; admission free; ⊙10am-6.30pm summer; ; Lido SME) looks like an alien landing. A series of ramps and staircases lead to a bar, a restaurant, a raised dance floor and a viewing platform. In summer the hive-like structure hums with daytime events and activities.

4 Hit the Public Beach

This is the closest *spiaggia comunale* (public beach) to the ferry and on sunny weekends it can get packed. Spread out your towel on the sand with impunity; most other beaches on the island are commercialised, with rows of changing sheds and deck chairs for hire.

5 Happy Hour on El Pecador

No you're not suffering from heatstroke: that really is a red, double-decker bus parked along the Lungomare, attracting an alternative crowd to impromptu beach parties. Head to **El Pecador** (Lungomare Gabriele d'Annunzio; sandwiches €2.50-5; ⊙10am-2am Apr-Oct; Lido SME) for some of the Lido's finest stuffed sandwiches and *spritz* (prosecco cocktails), and claim a seat on the canopied top deck.

6 Party at Pachuka

The most reliable of the Lido's summertime dance spots, **Pachuka** (☎041 770 147; www.pachuka.it; Via Umberto Klinger; ⊙hours vary; Lido San Nicolò) works year-round as a snack bar and pizzeria but on summer weekend nights it cranks up as a beachside dance club, too. Expect live music and DJ sets right on the beach.

For reviews see
Top Sights p130
Sights p141
Eating p143
Drinking p146
Shopping p146

Basilica di Santa Maria Assunta
Chiesa di San Giorgio Maggiore
4 Cimitero di San Michele
Fondazione Giorgio Cini
Museo del Merletto
3 Monastero di San Lazzaro degli Armeni
5 Acquolina Cooking School
Stazione di Santa Lucia (Ferrovia)

Torcello
Burano
Mazzorbo
Murano
Sacca Serenella
Isola di San Michele
Giudecca
Sacca Fisola
Isola di San Giorgio Maggiore
Isola delle Certosa
Le Vignole
Sant'Erasmo
Lido di Venezia
Litorale di Sant'Erasmo
Punta Sabbioni
Isola di San Servolo
Isola di San Clemente
Isola del Lazzaretto Vecchio
Isola delle Rose
Isola di Sant'Angelo
Isola di San Giorgio in Alga
Isola di Tresse
Isola del Tronchetto
Isola di San Secondo
Isola di Campalto
Isola di Tessera
Isola Carbonera
Punta Langa
Isola Buel del Lovo
Isola della Madonna del Monte
Isola di San Giacomo in Palude
Isola del Lazzaretto Nuovo
Isola di San Francesco del Deserto
Ponte della Libertà
Porto Marghera
Porto di Campalte
Porto del Lido
Canale di Treporti
Canale di Burano
Canale della Giudecca
Canale di San Marco
Grand Canal
Canale Osellino
Palude del Monte
Palude di Centrega
Via Orlanda
Via Fausta
Fusina
Venezia
Laguna

0 — 2 km
0 — 1 mile

Labyrinth, Fondazione Giorgio Cini

Sights

Fondazione Giorgio Cini

CULTURAL CENTRE

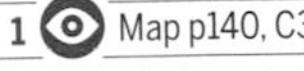
1 Map p140, C3

In 1951, industrialist and art patron Vittorio Cini – a survivor of Dachau – acquired the monastery of San Giorgio and restored it in memory of his son, Giorgio Cini. The rehabilitated complex is an architectural treasure incorporating designs by Palladio and Baldassare Longhena. Weekend tours allow you to stroll through a garden labyrinth and contemplate the tranquil Cypress Cloister, the oldest extant part of the complex (1526). Check the website for exhibitions, events and performances in the open-air Teatro Verde. (☎347 3386426; www.cini.it; Isola di San Giorgio Maggiore; adult/reduced €10/8; ⏱tours 10am-5pm Sat & Sun; ⛴San Giorgio Maggiore)

Museo del Merletto

MUSEUM

2  Map p140, E1

Burano's Lace Museum tells the story of a craft that cut across social boundaries, endured for centuries and evoked the epitome of civilisation reached during the Republic's heyday. From the triple-petalled corollas on the fringes of the Madonna's mantle in Torcello's 12th-century mosaics to Queen Margherita's spider-web-fine 20th-century mittens, lace-making was both the creative expression of female sensitivity and a highly lucrative craft. (Lace Museum; 041 73 00 34; www.museomerletto.visitmuve.it; Piazza Galuppi 187, Burano; adult/reduced €5/3.50, with Museum Pass free; 10am-5pm; Burano)

Monastero di San Lazzaro degli Armeni MONASTERY

3 Map p140, C4

Tours of the historic Armenian island monastery start in its glittering church and are conducted by multilingual monks, who amply demonstrate the institution's reputation for scholarship. After passing through the 18th-century refectory, you'll head upstairs to the library. In 1789 the monks set up a polyglot printing press here and translated many scientific and literary works into Armenian. Those works are still housed in the 150,000-strong collection alongside curios from Ancient Egypt, Sumeria and India. (041 526 01 04; Isola di San Lazzaro degli Armeni; adult/reduced €6/4.50; tours 3.25pm; San Lazzaro)

Local Life

Boating on the Lagoon

Terra e Acqua (347 4205004; www.veneziainbarca.it; day trips from €400) offers wild rides to the outer edges of the lagoon on a sturdy motorised *bragozzo* (flat-bottomed fishing vessel) accommodating up to 12 people. Itineraries are customised, and can cover abandoned quarantine islands and the hard-to-reach friary on Isola di San Francesco del Deserto.

For those who like to be in charge of their own destiny, **Venice Kayak** (346 4771327; www.venicekayak.com; Vento di Venezia, Isola della Certosa; half-/full-day tours €90/120) organises well-planned tours in the warren of Venice's canals and out to remote islands in the broad garden of the lagoon.

Cimitero di San Michele CEMETERY

4 Map p140, C3

Until Napoleon established a city cemetery on this little island, Venetians had been buried in parish plots across town – not an ideal solution in a watery city. Today, goths, incorrigible romantics and music lovers pause here to pay respects to Ezra Pound, Joseph Brodsky, Sergei Diaghilev and Igor Stravinsky. Pick up a map from the information point near the entrance and join them, but be aware, the map pinpointing of the famous graves isn't accurate. (Isola di San Michele; admission free; 7.30am-6pm Apr-Sep, to 4.30pm Oct-Mar; Cimitero)

Acquolina Cooking School COOKING

5 Map p140, D4

These intimate cookery classes are held by Marika Contaldo in her flower-festooned Lido villa. Serious gourmets will want to consider the multiday culinary vacations, which include cookery lessons interspersed with market visits, lagoon cruises and trips to the Segusa glass factory. Otherwise, there are half- and full-day taster courses, the latter including a morning trip to the Rialto Market. (041 526 72 26; www.acquolina.com; Via Lazzaro Mocenigo 10, Lido; half-/full-day courses €170/290; ; Lido)

Eating

Trattoria Altanella VENETIAN €€

6 Map p140, C4

Founded by a fisherman and his wife in 1920 and still run by the same family, this cosy restaurant serves fine Venetian fare such as potato gnocchi with cuttlefish and perfectly grilled fish. Inside, the vintage interior is hung with artworks, reflecting the restaurant's popularity with artists, poets and writers, while outside a flower-fringed balcony hangs over the canal. (041 522 77 80; Calle de le Erbe 268, Giudecca; meals €38-47; 12.30-2.30pm & 7.30-10.30pm Wed-Sun; ; Redentore)

Locanda Cipriani VENETIAN €€€

7 Map p140, E1

Run by the Cipriani family since 1935, the Locanda is Harry's Bar gone rustic, with a wood-beamed dining room opening onto a pretty country garden. But standards are standards, so staff buzz about in dapper bow ties, theatrically silver serving every dish – even the pasta! The kitchen is just as precise, delivering pillowy gnocchi, perfectly cooked fish and decadent chocolate mousse. (041 73 01 50; www.locandacipriani.com; Piazza Torcello 29, Torcello; meals €53-69; noon-3pm Wed-Mon Mar-Dec, plus 6-11pm Fri & Sat Apr-Sep; Torcello)

Acquastanca MODERN ITALIAN €€

8  Map p140, C3

A modern sensibility imbues both the decor and the menu at this wonderful little restaurant. A knowing array of old-fashioned Murano mirrors adorns a wall, while birds perch on artfully arranged twigs on another. Seafood features prominently on a menu that includes fresh flavour-filled takes on the classic Venetian bean soup, octopus with chickpeas and a panoply of pasta. (041 319 51 25; www.acquastanca.it; Fondamenta Manin 48, Murano; meals €40-44; 10am-11pm Mon & Fri, 9am-8pm Tue-Thu & Sat summer, 10am-10pm Mon & Fri, 10am-4pm Tue-Thu & Sat winter; Faro)

La Palanca VENETIAN €€

9 Map p140, C4

Locals of all ages pour into this humble bar for *cicheti*, coffee and *spritz*. However, it's at lunchtime that it really comes into its own, serving surprisingly sophisticated fare like swordfish carpaccio with orange zest alongside more rustic dishes, such as a delicious thick seafood soup. In summer, competition for waterside tables is stiff. (041 528 77 19; Fondamenta Sant'Eufemia 448, Giudecca; meals €25-33; 7am-8pm Mon-Sat; Palanca)

Venissa Osteria
VENETIAN €€

10 Map p140, E1

More affordable than its Michelin-starred sister, this upmarket *osteria* (casual tavern) offers updates on Venetian classics such as marinated fish, duck pasta and *bigoli* (thick wholemeal pasta with anchovies). For an extra treat, splash out on a glass of Dorona, the prestigious golden-hued wine varietal only grown here. Make sure you save room for some of Venice's best desserts. (041 527 22 81; www.venissa.it; Fondamenta Santa Caterina 3, Mazzorbo; meals €40-47; noon-6pm Wed, Thu, Sun & Mon, noon-midnight Fri & Sat Apr-Oct; Mazzorbo)

La Favorita
VENETIAN, SEAFOOD €€

11 Map p140, D4

La Favorita has been delivering long, lazy lunches, bottles of fine wine and impeccable service since 1955. The menu is full of traditional Venetian seafood dishes such as *rombo* (turbot) simmered with cherry tomatoes and olives, crab *gnochetti* (mini-gnocchi) and classic fish risotto. (041 526 16 26; Via Francesco Duodo 33, Lido; meals €38-53; 12.30-2.30pm & 7-10.30pm Fri-Sun, 7-10.30pm Tue-Thu; Lido San Nicolò)

Osteria al Duomo
ITALIAN €€

12 Map p140, C2

Opened in 1903 by the parish priest as a co-op grocery shop, this *osteria* is still collectively owned by 50 Muranese families. Don't be surprised, then, by the honest bowls of pasta and hands-down the best pizza in Venice – as you'd expect, considering the furnace they have to cook them in! In summer, sit out in the walled garden. (041 527 43 03; www.osteriaalduomo.com; Fondamenta Maschio 20-21, Murano; meals €27-43; 11am-10pm; ; Museo)

Understand

Venissa: A Mazzorbo Renaissance

In 1999, Gianluca Bisol, a *prosecco* producer from Valdobbiadene, heard of an ancient vineyard enclosed by medieval walls on Mazzorbo. He rented the land from the city and set about rehabilitating the rare Renaissance Dorona grape from just 88 vines which had survived.

Once he'd reclaimed the Venissa vineyard, he turned his attention to the buildings, which he converted into a six-room **guesthouse** and an **osteria**. Since then a Michelin-starred restaurant**, Venissa Ristorante** (041 527 22 81; www.venissa.it; Fondamenta Santa Caterina 3, Mazzorbo; 6-course menu €120; 12.30-4pm & 7-10pm Wed-Mon Apr-Oct; Mazzorbo) has been added in the garden.

The entire operation is now managed by Gianluca's son Matteo, and his latest project has been the opening of Casa Burano (p175), an *albergo diffuso* (multi-venue hotel) with 13 rooms spread through five cottages on Burano.

KEVIN GALVIN/ALAMY ©

Canalside cafe on the Lido

Magiche Voglie GELATO €

13 Map p140, D4

The best ice cream in the Lido is made every morning on the premises at this family-owned gelateria. Mull over the soft peaks of new-world flavours such as acai berry and caja fruit, or plump for the classic purplish-black cherry or Sicilian pistachio. (Gran Viale Santa Maria Elisabetta 47g, Lido; cones €2.50-4.50; 10am-11.30pm summer; Lido SME)

Trattoria al Gatto Nero SEAFOOD €€€

14 Map p140, E1

Once you've tried the homemade *tagliolini* with spider crab, whole grilled fish and perfect house-baked biscuits, the ferry ride to Burano seems a minor inconvenience – a swim back here from Venice would be worth it for the mixed seafood grill alone. Call ahead and plead for canalside seating. (041 73 01 20; www.gattonero.com; Fondamenta della Giudecca 88, Burano; meals €43-70; noon-3pm & 7.30-10pm Tue-Sun; Burano)

Trattoria ai Cacciatori VENETIAN €€

15 Map p140, C4

If you hadn't guessed from the oversized gun hanging from the ceiling beams, the restaurant is named for the hunters who once bagged lagoon waterfowl. Dishes are hearty but sophisticated, including both game and local seafood. (☎328 736 33 46; www.aicacciatori.it; Fondamenta del Ponte Piccolo 320, Giudecca; meals €40-47; ⏰noon-3pm & 6.30-10pm Tue-Sun; ⛴Palanca)

Drinking

Skyline

ROOFTOP BAR

16 Map p140, B3

From white-sneaker cruise passengers to the €300-sunglasses set, the rooftop bar at the Hilton Molino Stucky wows everyone with its vast panorama over Venice and the lagoon. DJs spin tunes on Friday night year-round and on additional nights in summer, when the action moves to the deck and pool. There's occasional live music too. (☎041 272 33 11; www.skylinebarvenice.com; Fondamenta San Biagio 810, Giudecca; ⏰5pm-1am; ⛴Palanca)

Local Life

Regatta Revelry

The biggest event in the northern lagoon calendar is the 32km **Vogalonga long row** (www.vogalonga.com) from Venice to Murano and back each May. It's a fabulously festive occasion when hundreds of enthusiasts take to the waters in their wooden *batèla* (flat-bottomed boats) and motorised boats are banned from the lagoon for the day.

Plan in advance and find a grassy picnic spot on Mazzorbo. If you'd like to have a go yourself get in touch with Row Venice (p106).

Villa Laguna

BAR

17 Map p140, D4

Sunset photo ops don't come any better than on the terrace of Villa Laguna. This restored, Habsburg holiday chalet is the only lagoon-facing hotel on the Lido and its west-facing terrace and lounge bar guarantees views of San Marco framed by a blushing pink sky. (☎041 526 13 16; www.hotelvillalaguna.com; Via Sandro Gallo 6, Lido; ⏰7-10pm Tue-Sun; ⛴Lido)

Caffè-Bar Palmisano

CAFE

18 Map p140, E1

Refuel with espresso and a toasted sandwich at this cafe on the sunny side of the street, and return later to celebrate photo-safari triumphs over *spritz* or wine with regular crowds of fishermen and university students. (Via Galuppi 351, Burano; ⏰7am-9pm; ⛴Burano)

Shopping

Emilia

ARTS & CRAFTS

Doyenne Emilia di Ammendola, a third-generation lace-maker, has passed on her skills to her son and daughter who are continuing the family tradition in this flagship store, located near the Lace Museum (see **2** Map p44, E8). There are also branches in London and LA, and a partnership with Austin Martin. Prices befit the quality (ie out of this world), but you can take away a tiny souvenir for €10. Upstairs there's a

Top Tip

A Spa with a View

Set on a 16-hectare private island, 20 minutes from Piazza San Marco, JW Marriott's Venetian **hotel** (041 852 13 00; www.jwvenice.com; Isola delle Rose; d €360-485; spa 9.30am-8pm;) is a bucolic haven in the lagoon. While Matteo Thun's contemporary, minimalist interiors and rooms are elegant in the extreme, it's the **rooftop spa and pools** (indoor and outdoor), with their four-poster loungers and unimpeded views across the lagoon, that really steal the show.

Non-hotel guests can access the island via the free shuttle from San Marco Giardinetti. Even the basic package offering use of the facilities is worth the trip, otherwise there are a range of massages (€125 to €170), hammam treatments (€90) and even a Michelin-starred restaurant.

family museum. (041 73 52 99; www.emiliaburano.it; Via Galuppi 205, Burano; 9.30am-7pm; Burano)

Fornace Mian GLASS

19 Map p140, C2

Shuffle past the typical Murano kitsch (parrots in trees etc) and you'll find one of the best ranges of classic stemware on the island. Samples are displayed in the showroom but everything's made to order and takes about 10 days to produce. Either call in early on in your trip, or arrange them to ship your purchases home. (041 73 94 23; www.fornacemian.com; Fondamenta da Mula 143, Murano; 9.30am-5.30pm; Venier)

Cartavenezia ARTS & CRAFTS

20 Map p140, B4

Paper is anything but two-dimensional here: paper maestro Fernando di Masone embosses and sculpts handmade cotton paper into seamless raw-edged lampshades, hand-bound sketchbooks, and paper versions of marble friezes that would seem equally at home in a Greek temple or a modern loft. White gloves are handy for easy, worry-free browsing; paper-sculpting courses are available by prior request. (041 524 12 83; www.cartavenezia.it; Campo di S Cosmo 621f, Giudecca; by appointment; Palanca)

Salvadore GLASS

21 Map p140, C2

This store specialises in light-hearted creations, including multicoloured drinking glasses and bead necklaces like strands of tiny beach balls. Aspiring designers can create their own looks from individual glass beads. (041 73 67 72; Fondamenta dei Vetrai 128a, Murano; 10.30am-6pm Mon-Sat; Colonna)

40

The Best of Venice

Venice's Best Walks

Venice's Best...

Colourful houses on Burano (p128)
TIPWAM/SHUTTERSTOCK ©

Best Walks **San Marco Royal Tour**

The Walk

Dukes and dignitaries had the run of San Marco for centuries, and now it's your turn on this royal tour that ends with your own palace intrigue.

Start Piazzetta San Marco

Finish Scala Contarini del Bovolo

Length 2.5km; 1¼ hours

Take a Break

Charming staff dispense delicious *cicheti* (Venetian tapas) from a central horseshoe-shaped bar in upmarket little **Black-Jack** (p44).

Piazza San Marco and Basilica di San Marco (p24)

❶ Columns of San Marco

Venetians still hurry past these granite pillars, site of public executions for centuries.

❷ Palazzo Ducale

Pass by the **Ducal Palace** (p28) loggia, where punishments were once publicly announced before they were posted on the palace door.

❸ Piazza San Marco

In **Piazza San Marco**, turn your back on the **Basilica di San Marco** (p24) to face Ala Napoleonica, the palace Napoleon brazenly razed San Geminiano church to build. Today it houses the entry to the **Museo Correr** (p36); the museum proper occupies the upper storeys of the Scamozzi-designed, Longhena-completed Procuratie Nuove. The right-hand arcade flanking the piazza is Mauro Codussi's 16th-century Procuratie Vecchie.

❹ Chiesa di Santa Maria del Giglio

Take Calle Larga XXII Marzo towards this baroque **church** (p38), sculpted with maps of Rome and five cities that were Venetian possessions at the time.

❺ Chiesa di Santo Stefano

Stop to admire Bartolomeo Bon's marble Gothic portals as you walk past **St Steven's Church** (p37), and then continue around to the Campo Sant'Anzolo and look back. The church's free-standing bell tower leans 2m, as though it's had one *spritz* too many.

❻ La Fenice

After pausing to take note of Venice's famous opera house, **La Fenice** (p44), take canyon-like Calle de la Verona into the shadows and continue on to Calle dei Assassini. Corpses were so frequently found here that in 1128, Venice banned the full beards assassins wore as disguises.

❼ Scala Contarini del Bovolo

Snogging in *campi* (squares) is such an established Venetian pastime it's surprising doges didn't tax it – but duck into Renaissance **Scala Contarini del Bovolo** (p38) courtyard for privacy.

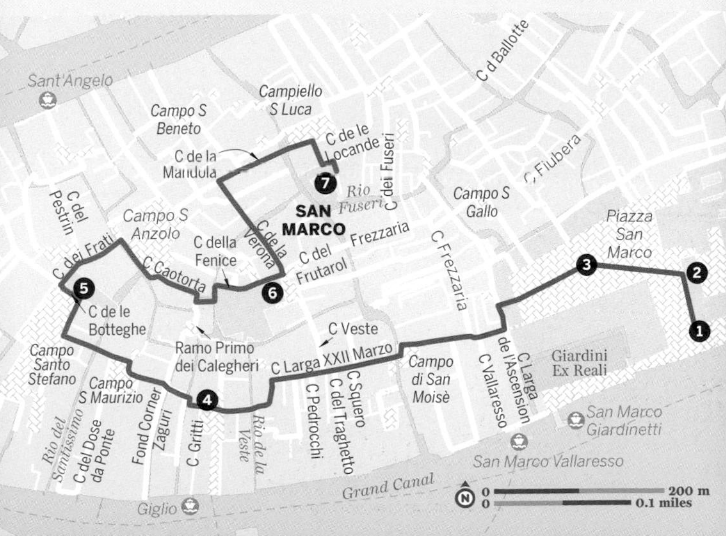

Best Walks
Venice Culinary Adventure

The Walk

Before there were painters, opera divas or doges in Venice, there were fishmongers and grocers at the Rialto, bragging shamelessly about their wares. Today, the trade-route cuisine they inspired fills this corner of Venice with delectable discoveries for all your senses. Follow your growling stomach to find them on this culinary walking tour.

Start Rialto Market

Finish Al Prosecco

Length 3.25km; two hours

Take a Break

Duck into **All'Arco** (p82) for the city's best *cicheti* (Venetian tapas) – ask for *una fantasia* (a fantasy), and father-son chefs Francesco and Matteo will invent a dish with ingredients you just saw at the market.

❶ Rialto Market

A trip through gourmet history starts at this **market** (p74), with its roofed Pescaria, where fishmongers artfully arrange the day's catch atop hillocks of ice.

❷ Drogheria Mascari

Glimpse trade-route treasures that made Venice's fortune at this gourmet **showcase** (p90). Spice pyramids grace shop windows, while speciality sweets are dispensed from copper-topped apothecary jars.

❸ Casa del Parmigiano

Displays of local San Daniele ham and Taleggio cheese at **Casa del Parmigiano** (p90) are reminders that Veneto's culinary fame wasn't built on seafood and spices alone.

❹ Cárte

Wander northwest to this tiny **studio-boutique** (p92) to browse lagoon-rippled, marble-paper recipe albums, and dress for dinner with paper cocktail rings.

❺ Veneziastampa

Cross a couple of bridges until you smell ink drying on letterpress menus and cookbook ex libris labels at **Veneziastampa** (p89).

❻ Museo di Storia Naturale di Venezia

Learn the scientific names of the lagoon creatures you spotted at the market at Venice's **museum of natural history** (p80), housed in a Grand Canal palace that was once the Turkish trading-house. It's filled with curious specimens, but architecture made from shellfish and fishbones steals the show.

❼ Riva di Biasio

Walk this sunny Grand Canal footpath allegedly named for 16th-century butcher Biagio (Biasio) Cargnio, whose sausages contained a special ingredient: children. When found out, Biasio was drawn and quartered.

❽ Gelato di Natura

Along with a dozen other things, Marco Polo is said to have introduced ice cream to Venice. At this **gelato shop** (p84) the experimentation continues with small-batch gelato incorporating organic ingredients such as Bronte pistachios, Piedmontese hazlenuts and Amalfi lemons.

❾ Al Prosecco

Happy-hour temptations ring nearby Campo San Giacomo dell'Orio, but gourmet adventures deserve natural-process *prosecco* (sparkling wine) toasts at **Al Prosecco** (p86).

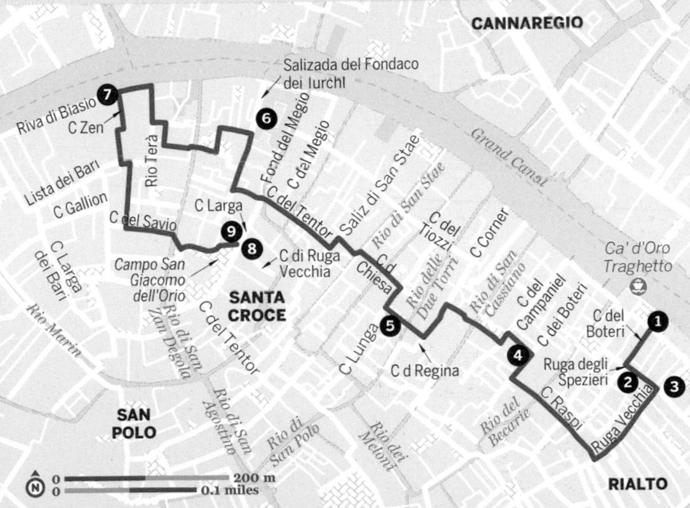

Best Walks Castello's Byways

The Walk

Leave the crowds and cramped quarters of San Marco behind, and stretch your legs on a sunny stroll through Castello, where saints and sailors come with the territory.

Start Zanipolo (Chiesa di SS Giovanni e Paolo)

Finish Giardini Pubblici

Length 6.5km; three hours

Take a Break

After your walk, enjoy a heavenly herbal tisane inside Napoleon's greenhouse at **Serra dei Giardini** (p124) – or a sailor-size *spritz* (*prosecco* cocktail) and lagoon-front seat to watch boats drift past at **Paradiso** (041 241 39 72; Giardini Pubblici 1260; 9am-7pm, later during Biennale; Giardini Biennale).

ROSTISLAV GLINSKY/SHUTTERSTOCK ©

Arsenale

1 Zanipolo

Rising above Castello's tallest ship-masts is Gothic **Zanipolo** (p116) basilica. Its 33m-high nave provides a fitting setting for 25 doges' tombs.

2 Ospedaletto

A block east, you can't miss statue-bedecked **Ospedaletto** (p126), a 1660s orphanage designed by Longhena. This refuge was once famed for its orchestra of orphan girls; today it functions as an elder-care facility.

3 Chiesa di San Francesco della Vigna

Continue down Barbaria delle Tole, then dog-leg left to see Palladio-colonnaded **Chiesa di San Francesco della Vigna** (p116), where Antonio Negroponte's Madonna and child float like a hovercraft above Venice's lagoon.

4 Arsenale

Heading south, you'll bump into the massive walls of the **Arsenale** (p119), Venice's legendary shipyard. Turn right at Campo de le Gorne and follow the walls to this **Chiesa di San Martino**, dedicated to St Martin, patron saint of wine and soldiers. By the doorway is a *bocca di leoni* (mouth of the lion), a slot where Venetians slipped denunciations of their neighbours. *Arsenalotti* (Arsenale workers) were sworn to silence about trade secrets, since loose lips could sink ships – so reckless talk in Castello bars could be reported as high treason, punishable by death.

❺ Porta Magna

The Arsenale's main gate is considered the city's earliest Renaissance structure. By the 18th century naval production at the Arsenale had dwindled and the republic was in terminal decline. In 1797 La Serenissima surrendered to Napoleon without a fight.

❻ Riva

From here, turn south onto Castello's breathtaking waterfront promenade to admire sweeping views across the lagoon.

❼ Giardini Pubblici

The Napoleonic **public gardens** (p116) are dotted with Biennale pavilions, thronged summer through fall with artists, architects and admirers from around the world. Between Biennales you can still enjoy the rest of the park.

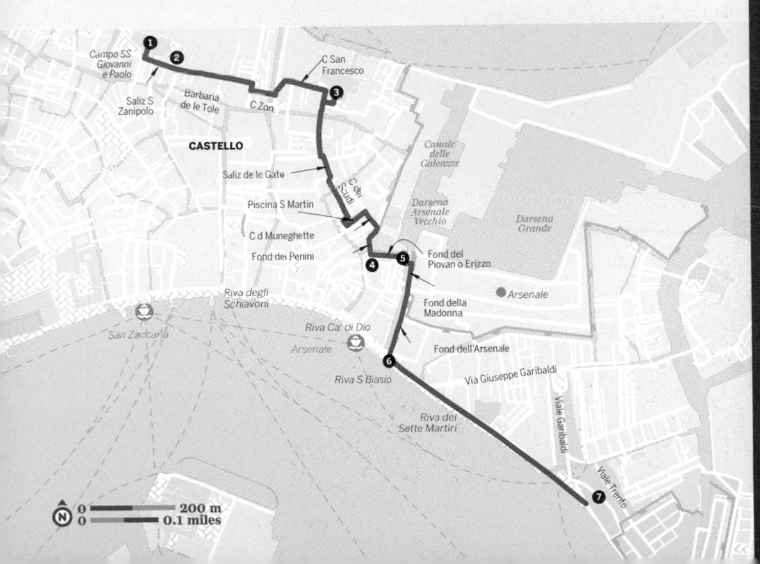

Best Eating

The visual blitz that is Venice tends to leave visitors weak-kneed and grasping for the nearest *panino* (sandwich). But there's more to La Serenissima than simple carb-loading. For centuries Venice has gone beyond the call of dietary duty, and lavished visitors with inventive feasts. Now it's your turn to devour addictive *cicheti* (Venetian tapas) and a lagoon's worth of succulent seafood.

Venetian Cuisine

Cross-cultural fusion fare is old news here, dating back to Marco Polo's heyday. Thirteenth-century Venetian cookbooks include recipes for fish with galangal, saffron and ginger; a tradition that still inspires dishes at nosh spots like Bistrot de Venise (p40) and Osteria Trefanti (p83). Don't be surprised if some dishes taste vaguely Turkish or Greek, reflecting Venice's trading partners for over a millennium. Spice-route flavours can be savoured in signature Venetian recipes such as *sarde in saor,* traditionally made with sardines in a tangy onion marinade with pine nuts and sultanas.

Cicheti

Cicheti are some of the best culinary finds in Italy, served at lunch and from around 6pm to 8pm. They range from basic bar snacks (spicy meatballs, fresh tomato and basil bruschetta) to highly inventive small plates. Prices start at €1 for tasty meatballs and range from €3 to €6 for gourmet fantasias with fancy ingredients.

STOCKSNAPPER/SHUTTERSTOCK ©

Top Tips

- If all that produce and tradition inspires the chef within, sign up for a Venetian cooking course. Acquolina Cooking School (p142) runs four- and eight-hour courses, the latter option including a morning trip to the Rialto Market. It also offers multiday courses, including accommodation.

Best Classic Venetian

Antiche Carampane Excellent seafood and moreish *fritto misto* (fried seafood) in Venice's former red-light corner. (p82)

Cicheti (Venetian tapas)

Trattoria Altanella Authentic Venetian recipes served up by the same family since 1920. (p143)

Da Codroma Venetian dishes accredited by Slow Food. (p61)

Best Inventive Venetian

Venissa Graze on the island landscape in lagoon-inspired dishes by rising culinary talents. (p144)

Ristorante Glam A modern take on Venetian classics from a Michelin-starred chef. (p83)

CoVino A pocket-sized showcase for Slow Food produce. (p120)

Estro Gourmet *cicheti* and highly creative Venetian cooking. (p60)

Best Cicheti

All'Arco Market-fresh morsels and zingy *prosecco* close to the Rialto Market. (p82)

Vino Vero Inventive bar snacks accompanied by natural-process wines. (p99)

Dai Zemei Unexpected, creative concoctions from food- and wine-obsessed twins. (p83)

Best Waterfront Dining

Trattoria Altanella Wine, dine and sigh on a balcony that hovers right over the water. (p143)

Riviera Perfectly positioned on the Zattere for hot-pink sunsets and romance. (p60)

La Palanca Panoramic waterfront dining at mere-mortal prices. (p143)

Best Cheap Eats

All'Arco Stand-up gourmet bites made with prime Rialto produce. (p82)

Snack Bar Ai Nomboli Inspired sandwiches made with quality ingredients. (p84)

Pasticceria Tonolo The best pastry shop in Venice. (p61)

Didovich An all-day eatery with outstanding outdoor seating. (p121)

Best Drinking

When the siren sounds for *acqua alta* (high tide), Venetians close up shop and head home to put up their flood barriers – then pull on their boots and head right back out again. Why let floods disrupt a toast? It's not just a turn of phrase: come hell or high water, Venetians will find a way to have a good time.

What to Order

No rules seem to apply to drinking in Venice. No mixing spirits and wine? Venice's classic cocktails suggest otherwise; try a *spritz* (pictured right), made with *prosecco,* soda water and bittersweet Aperol, bitter Campari or herbaceous Cynar. Price is not an indicator of quality – you can pay €2.50 for a respectable *spritz,* or live to regret that €16 bellini tomorrow (ouch). If you're not pleased with your drink, leave it and move on to the next *bacaro* (bar). Don't be shy about asking fellow drinkers what they recommend; happy hour is a highly sociable affair.

DOC Versus IGT

In Italy, the official DOC *(denominazione d'origine controllata)* and elite DOCG (DOC *garantita* – guaranteed) designations are assurances of top-notch *vino*. Yet, successful as its wines are, the Veneto also bucks the DOC/DOCG system. Many of the region's small-production wineries can't be bothered with such external validation as they already sell out to Venetian bars and restaurants. As a result, some top producers prefer the IGT *(indicazione geografica tipica)* designation, which guarantees grapes typical of the region but leaves winemakers room to experiment.

WJAREK/SHUTTERSTOCK ©

Best Wine Bars

Vino Vero Natural, biodynamic and boutique drops in a standout Cannaregio wine bar. (p99)

Al Prosecco A showcase of Italy's finest natural-process wines and biodynamic viticulture. (p86)

Ai Pugni Nightly canalside crowds and a long, interesting, ever-changing choice of *vino* by the glass. (p64)

Timon Top-class wines by the glass and live music sets canalside. (p99)

Enoteca Mascareta Inspired wines by the glass, including

Left: *Spritz*; Right: Vino Vero (p99)

the owner's very own organic *prosecco*. (p123)

Best for Beer

Birre da Tutto il Mondo o Quasi Venice's top beer bar keeps punters purring with over 100 brews. (p109)

La Cantina House-brand beer Gaston is a winner with sud-loving locals. (p108)

Il Santo Bevitore Trappist ales, seasonal stouts and chat-igniting football matches on the TV. (p107)

Best Signature Cocktails

Harry's Bar The driest classic in town is Harry's gin-heavy martini – no olive. (p43)

Locanda Cipriani Harry's famous white-peach bellini tastes even better at Cipriani's island retreat. (p143)

Bar Longhi Drink top-class cocktails like the orange martini in a jewel-like interior. (p42)

Bar Terrazza Danieli Apricot and orange moonlight with gin and grenadine in the Danieli. (p123)

Best Cafes

Caffè Florian An 18th-century time-warp in show-off Piazza San Marco. (p33)

Grancaffè Quadri This baroque bar-cafe has been serving punters since 1699. (p42)

Torrefazione Cannaregio A veteran coffee roaster famed for its hazelnut-laced espresso. (p108)

Caffè del Doge A serious selection of world coffees, including the rare kopi luwak. (p87)

Best For Kids

Adults think Venice is for them; kids know better. This is where every fairy tale comes to life, where prisoners escape through the roof of a pink palace, Murano glass-blowers breathe life into pocket-sized sea dragons, and spellbound Pescaria fish balance on their tails as though spellbound.

Best Family-Friendly Attractions

Palazzo Ducale Explore a Gothic prison on the Secret Itineraries tour. (p28)

Torre dell'Orologio Climb this clock tower for giddy views of the bell-chiming *automata*. (pictured right; p37)

Museo di Storia Naturale di Venezia Discover dinosaurs, mummies and adventures on the high seas. (p80)

Lido Beaches Sandy beaches and shallow waters make for a perfect escape. (p138)

Best Hands-On Learning

Row Venice Hop on and learn to row as gondoliers do. (p106)

Ca' Macana Be inspired and craft your own Carnevale mask. (p65)

Acquolina Cooking School Get to grips with sci-fi-looking lagoon creatures. (p142)

Venice Italian School Learn to order gelato like a pro. (p84)

Best Child-Friendly Dining

Caffè Florian Hot chocolate in fairy-tale interiors. (p33)

Rosticceria Gislon Perennially popular roast chicken in a 1930s canteen. (p42)

Serra dei Giardini Napoleon's greenhouse is a perfect pit stop for tea and cake. (p124)

Osteria al Duomo Great pizza in a walled garden on Murano. (p144)

Suso Top-notch gelato made from organic ingredients. (p42)

Top Tips

▶ Given the expense of eating out, many families find that opting for an apartment is a life saver. Not only will you have your own kitchen, but the experience of shopping at the Rialto is a memorable cultural experience. Views on Venice (p175) have a good selection of family-friendly apartments to choose from.

Best Museums

Peek inside Grand Canal palaces donated to Venice, and you'll find they're packed to attic rafters with Prada couture, samurai armour and the odd dinosaur. Though he tried for 11 years, Napoleon couldn't steal all the treasures Venetians had hoarded for centuries. Generous benefactors have restored Venice's treasure-box museums and added plenty to them, too.

Best Venetian Blockbusters

Gallerie dell'Accademia Watch Venetian painters set the world ablaze with saturated colour and censorship-defying art. (p50)

Palazzo Ducale The doge's home decor is the world's prettiest propaganda, featuring Veronese, Tintoretto, Tiepolo and Titian. (pictured right; p28)

Museo Correr Palace rooms dedicated to pink Bellinis and blood-red Carpaccios, plus philosophers by Veronese, Titian and Tintoretto in the library. (p36)

Scuola Grande di San Rocco Tintoretto upstages Veronese with action-packed scenes of angelic rescue squads. (p70)

Ca' d'Oro Baron Franchetti's treasure-box palace packed with masterpieces. (p102)

Best Fashion-Forward Palaces

Museo Fortuny The radical fashion house that freed women from corsets keeps raising eyebrows. (p36)

Fondazione Prada Futurist suits, video art and Duchamp suitcases are making waves along the Grand Canal inside stately Renaissance palace Ca' Corner. (p80)

Palazzo Mocenigo Find fashion inspiration in this palace packed with Venetian glamour. (p80)

Best Modern Art Museums

Peggy Guggenheim Collection Pollock, Rothko, Kandinsky and company make a splash on the Grand Canal. (p52)

Palazzo Grassi Murakami's manic daisies, Damien Hirst's shipwrecked treasures and other provocations in a Grand Canal palace. (p36)

Ca' Pesaro Klimts, Kandinskys and other modern masterpieces Venice slyly snapped up at the Biennale. (p80)

Punta della Dogana Mega-installations are docked inside Venice's ex-customs warehouses. (p58)

Best Architecture

From glittering Byzantine churches to post-modern palaces, Venice astonishes at every gondola turn. Its 1000-year architectural history has several high-water marks: pointy Venetian Gothic arches rounded off in the Renaissance; Palladio-revived rigorous classicism amid baroque flourishes; and stark modernism relaxing around decadent Lido Liberty (art nouveau).

Contemporary Venice

Despite the constraints of history, a surprising number of projects have turned Venice into a portfolio of contemporary architecture.

MIT-trained Italian architect Cino Zucchi kicked off the creative revival of Giudecca in 1995 with his conversion of 19th-century warehouses into art spaces and studio lofts. Since then London-based firm David Chipperfield Architects has breathed new life into the cemetery island of San Michele. Meanwhile, rebirth of the artistic kind underscores Fondazione Giorgio Cini's redevelopment into a global cultural centre. Across the canal Venice's historic Arsenale shipyards has seen its sheds turned into Biennale art galleries.

In addition, French art collector François Pinault hired Japanese architect Tadao Ando to repurpose Palazzo Grassi and the Punta della Dogana into settings for his contemporary-art collection, while Renzo Piano reinvented the Magazzini del Sale as a showcase for the Fondazione Vedova.

Culture and commerce co-exist in Dutch architect Rem Koolhaas' redevelopment of the Fondaco dei Tedeschi. Once a base for German merchants, the 16th-century *palazzo* (mansion) now houses a department store and a publicly accessible rooftop.

ANDREAS POLITIS/SHUTTERSTOCK ©

Best Divine Architecture

Basilica di San Marco Byzantine domes glimmer with golden mosaics. (pictured above; p24)

Basilica di Santa Maria della Salute Longhena's bubble-domed marvel, believed to have mystical curative powers. (p58)

Basilica di San Giorgio Maggiore Palladio's expansive, effortlessly uplifting church and cloisters. (p130)

I Frari A Gothic brick fancy with a scalloped roofline and a 14th-century *campanile* (bell tower). (p72)

Chiesa di Santa Maria dei Miracoli The Lombardos' little Renaissance miracle in polychrome marble. (p102)

Left: Dome of Basilica di San Marco (p24); Right: Chiesa di Santa Maria dei Miracoli (p102)

Schola Spagnola The theatrical, elliptical women's gallery attributed to Longhena. (p97)

Best Pleasure Palaces

Ca' d'Oro The grandest palace on the Grand Canal, with Venetian Gothic trilobate (three-lobed) arches and tiara-like crenelllation. (p102)

Palazzo Ducale Don't be fooled by Antonio da Ponte's pretty pink Gothic loggia: this palace was the seat of Venetian power. (p28)

Ca' Rezzonico Renaissance grandeur gone baroque: designed by Longhena, finished by Massari and crowned with Tiepolo ceilings. (p58)

Palazzo Grassi Gae Aulenti and Tadao Ando peeled back rococo flourishes to reveal Giorgio Massari's neoclassical lines. (p36)

Fondazione Querini Stampalia Baroque beauty with high-modernist updates: Carlo Scarpa–designed gardens and gates, Mario Botta library and cafe. (p117)

Best Modern Marvels

Biennale Pavilions High-modernist pavilion architecture – it may not sound like much, but it quite often steals the show at Art Biennales (p116)

Punta della Dogana A former customs warehouses creatively repurposed into cutting-edge installation-art galleries by Tadao Ando. (p58)

Negozio Olivetti Forward-thinking Carlo Scarpa transformed a dusty souvenir shop into a high-tech showcase c 1958. (p40)

Fondazione Giorgio Cini Former naval academy rocks the boat as an avant-garde art gallery. (p141)

Best Art

Water may be the first thing you notice about Venice when you arrive, but as you get closer, you'll discover that this city is actually saturated with art. Canals are just brief interruptions between artworks in this Unesco World Heritage Site, with more art treasures than any other city. Through censorship, plague and nonstop parties, Venice kept creating masterpieces.

COMMON PLACES, 2017, MARTIN CORDIANO
PHOTO BY: ANDREA AVEZZU. COURTESY: LA BIENNALE DI VENEZIA

☑ Top Tips

▸ See more art for less: get the 16-church **Chorus Pass** (adult/student under 29 years €12/8) or the **Civic Museum Pass** (adult/reduced €24/18), which is valid for six months and covers entry to 11 civic museums, including Palazzo Ducale, Ca' Rezzonico, Ca' Pesaro and the Museo Correr.

Best Venetian Masterpieces

Gallerie dell'Accademia Veronese's triumph over censorship: *Feast in the House of Levi*. (p50)

I Frari Titian's red-hot Madonna altarpiece: *Assunta*. (p72)

Scuola Grande di San Rocco Tintoretto to the rescue: *St Mark in Glory*. (p70)

Scuola Dalmata di San Giorgio degli Schiavoni Home to Carpaccio's delightful cycle of paintings of Dalmatian saints George, Tryphone and Jerome. (p116)

Basilica di Santa Maria Assunta Byzantine craftsmen spell out the consequences of dodging biblical commandments in the *Last Judgment.* (p132)

Ca' Pesaro *La Fanciulla del Fiore* by Gino Rossi. (p80)

Best Modern Art Showcases

La Biennale di Venezia The world's most prestigious art showcase, held in even-numbered years. Past works have included *Common Ground,* by Martin Cordiano, pictured above. (p118)

Peggy Guggenheim Collection Explore the modern art that caused uproars and defined the 20th century. (p52)

Fondazione Giorgio Cini Peter Greenaway videos in Palladio cloisters and blockbuster shows in a naval academy. (p141)

Punta della Dogana Historical customs warehouses retrofitted for the future with installation art. (p58)

Fondazione Vedova Rotating exhibits powered by robots. (p60)

Casa dei Tre Oci Italian and international exhibitions of contemporary art and photography. (p137)

Best Romance

Traffic never seemed so romantic as at sunset in Venice, when arias echo under the Ponte dei Sospiri (Bridge of Sighs) from passing gondolas. Venice is purpose-built for romance, with slow boats and opera instead of honking cars and curses. You don't have to be Casanova – Venice makes every romantic gesture grand.

Best Bolt-Holes

Al Ponte Antico A Grand Canal hideaway worthy of Casanova. (p175)

Oltre Il Giardino Effortless elegance with a whimsical, artistic soul. (p175)

Best Romantic Gestures

Palazetto Bru Zane Lingering glances at concerts in a frescoed pleasure palace. (p89)

La Fenice Welling up at opera premieres. (p44)

JW Marriott Venice Lounge on chiffon-clad four-posters with peerless views of Venice. (p147)

Gondola rides A proposal…or at least a compelling proposition. (p178)

Best Wining & Dining

Ristorante Quadri Red damask walls, candles and Michelin-starred dining show the love. (p40)

El Chioschetto Outdoor seating on the Zattere with front row views of fuschia sunsets. (p63)

Antiche Carampane Grown-up date nights in an intimate dining room. (p82)

Locanda Cipriani A romantic summer escape with tables in a rose garden. (p143)

Bar Longhi Perfect cocktails in sexy surroundings with Grand Canal views. (p42)

Top Tips

- Plan romantic getaways in winter when the fog rolls in and Venice's historic interiors glitter in the soft light.
- Book tickets to the opera and concerts well ahead.
- Need some place special for a *prosecco* toast or proposal? Ask a gondolier – they're experts.

Best Shopping

Beyond the world-famous museums and architecture is Venice's best-kept secret: the shopping. No illustrious shopping career is complete without trolling Venice for one-of-a-kind, artisan-made finds. All those souvenir tees and kitschy masks are nothing more than the decoys for the amateurs. Dig deeper and you'll stumble across the prized stuff – genuine, local and nothing short of inspiring.

Studio Visits

For your travelling companions who aren't sold on shopping, here's a convincing argument: in Venice, it really is an educational experience. In backstreet artisans' studios, you can watch ancient techniques used to make strikingly modern *carta memorizzata* (marbled paper; pictured right) and Murano glass. Studios cluster together, so to find unique pieces, just wander key artisan areas: San Polo around Calle Seconda dei Saoneri; Santa Croce around Campo Santa Maria Mater Domini; San Marco along Frezzeria and Calle de la Botteghe; Dorsoduro around the Peggy Guggenheim Collection; and Murano.

Best Original Venice Souvenirs

Pied à Terre *Furlane* (gondolier shoes) in all the colours of the rainbow. (p77)

Gianni Basso Calling cards with the lion of San Marco. (p110)

Paolo Brandolisio Miniature *forcole* (carved gondola oarlocks). (p127)

Gilberto Penzo Scale-model gondolas. (p92)

Best Venetian Home Decor

Fortuny Tessuti Artistici Luxury, handmade textiles from an Italian style icon. (p136)

ElleElle Fetching sets of affordable hand-blown glass. (p135)

Left: *Carta memorizzata* (marbled paper); Right: Silks on display at Venetia Studium (p46)

Chiarastella Cattana Sophisticated linens to restyle every corner of your *palazzo*. (p45)

Madera Forward-thinking objects, from chopping blocks to floor lamps. (p65)

Best Venetian Fashion

L'Armadio di Coco Luxury Vintage Couture fashions of yesteryear at affordable prices. (p45)

Venetia Studium Delphos tunic dresses and hand-stamped silk-velvet purses. (p46)

Venetian Dreams Lagoon-inspired swirling necklaces made with antique seed beads. (p47)

Emilio Ceccato The official supplier of natty gondolier gear. (p93)

Best Antiques

Ballarin A treasure chest packed with period furniture, lamps, glass and more. (p127)

Antiquariato Claudia Canestrelli A walk-in curiosity cabinet. (p66)

Antichità al Ghetto A nostalgic mix of Venetian maps, art and jewellery. (p111)

Best Jewellery

Oh My Blue Cutting-edge creations from local and foreign designers. (p76)

Marina e Susanna Sent Striking, contemporary wearables good enough for MoMA. (p65)

Best Leather Goods

Atelier Segalin di Daniela Ghezzo Custom-made shoes created with rare leather and seasoned style. (p46)

Balducci Borse Shoes and bags from a master leather craftsman. (p111)

Kalimala Natural tanning and top-shelf leather underlines goods for men and women. (p126)

Murra Embossed journals and leather satchels hand stamped with the Lion of St Mark. (p77)

Best Entertainment

Since the fall of its shipping empire, Venice has lived by its wits. No one throws a party like Venice, from Carnevale masquerades to Regata Storica floating parades – plus live opera, baroque music and jazz year-round, and summer movie premieres and beach concerts.

DEJAN_K/SHUTTERSTOCK ©

Festivals

If you'd survived the plague and Austrian invasion, you'd throw parties too – Venice celebrates with November's Festa della Madonna della Salute and July's Festa del Redentore. Regatta season from May's Vogalonga (www.vogalonga.com) to September's Regata Storica (www.regatastoricavenezia.it) sees cheering crowds along canal banks.

The Venice International Film Festival runs from the last weekend in August through the first week of September, bringing together international star power and Italian fashion.

Carnevale brings partying masqueraders (pictured right) on to the streets for two weeks preceding Lent. Tickets to La Fenice's masked balls run up to €230, but there are costume displays in every *campo* (square) and a Grand Canal flotilla to mark the start.

Live Music & Opera

A magnet for music fans for four centuries, Venice supplies a soundtrack of opera, classical music and jazz. You can still enjoy music as Venetians did centuries ago: La Fenice (p44) has been one of the world's top opera houses since 1792, while historical La Pietà (p126) orphanage is the original Vivaldi venue. Due to noise regulations in this small city with big echoes, shows typically end by 11pm.

☑ Top Tips

- For upcoming openings, concerts, performances, festivals and events, check accredited ticket seller www.veneziaunica.com.
- During Carnevale book accommodation well in advance and avoid the San Marco area which becomes extremely crowded.
- In summer bars and beach clubs on the Lido host concerts and club nights.

Left: Carnevale costumes; Right: La Fenice (p44)

Best Events

Carnevale (www.carnevale.venezia.it; January or February) Party in costume until wigs itch and livers twitch (about three weeks).

La Biennale di Venezia (www.labiennale.org; June to November) Outlandish openings in pavilions tricked out like surreal doll-houses. (p118)

Venice Jazz Festival (www.venetojazz.com; July) Jazz greats and the odd pop star play historical venues, including Piazza San Marco.

Venice International Film Festival (www.labiennale.org/it/cinema; August to September) Red carpets sizzle with star power, and deserving films actually win.

Venice Glass Week (www.theveniceglassweek.com; September) A week-long festival celebrating over a thousand years of artisanship.

Best Live Music

La Fenice Divas hit new highs in this historical jewel-box theatre. (p44)

Palazetto Bru Zane Leading interpreters of Romantic music raise the Sebastiano Ricci–frescoed roof. (p89)

Musica a Palazzo Operatic dramas unfold in a Grand Canal palace, from receiving-room overtures to bedroom grand finales. (p33)

Venice Music Gourmet Fine food in frescoed palaces with tunes from Vivaldi and Bach, as well as Italian jazz. (p122)

Best Local Favourites

Laboratorio Occupato Morion A radical backdrop for rocking regional bands. (p125)

Fondazione Giorgio Cini Occasionally serves up top-notch, modern world music. (p141)

Paradiso Perduto Jazz, salsa and the odd legend in an arty, old-school tavern. (p109)

Casa del Cinema Houses the film archive and screens art-house and independent films. (p89)

Best Secrets

Yellow signs across Venice helpfully point out major routes to San Marco, Rialto and Ferrovia (train station). But here's the secret to any great Venetian adventure: ignore those signs. Venice's finest moments are hidden in crooked *calli* (lanes), shady *cortili* (courtyards) and *palazzo* (palace) attics. Look no further for Venice's best artisans studios, finest seafood, spy headquarters and walk-in ball-gown closets.

Freebies

Despite its centuries-old reputation as a playground for Europe's elite, Venice's finest moments are freebies. Golden glimpses of heaven in the Basilica di San Marco are gratis as are theatrical displays at the Rialto Market. Entry is also free and potentially curative at the Basilica di Santa Maria della Salute, built as thanks for Venice's salvation from the plague, with a dome said to radiate healing energy. Carnevale is best celebrated in the streets – especially on the first weekend, when a massive costumed flotilla makes its way from the Rio di Cannaregio down the Grand Canal.

Art lovers will appreciate the superb (and often free) shows at Palazzo Franchetti (p38). Commercial art galleries and Murano glass showrooms are yours to enjoy at no cost, and state-run museums such as the Gallerie dell'Accademia and Ca' d'Oro are gratis on the first Sunday of the month. Then there is Venice's spectacular architecture: take in 50 Grand Canal mansions for the mere price of a *vaporetto* (ferry) ticket.

ALBERTO MASNOVO/SHUTTERSTOCK ©

Best Hidden Wonders

Chiesa di San Francesco della Vigna All-star Venetian art showcase and Palladio's first commission. (p116)

Chiesa di Santa Maria dei Miracoli The little neighbourhood church with big Renaissance ideas and priceless marble. (p102)

Museo di Storia Naturale di Venezia Dinosaurs, mummies and other bizarre scientific specimens brought home by intrepid Venetian explorers – all inside a Turkish fortress. (p80)

Basilica di Santa Maria Assunta Lambs bleat encouragement as you walk through this overgrown island towards golden glory in apse mosaics. (p132)

Left: Scala Contarini del Bovolo (p38); Right: Sculpture on the facade of the Palazzo Ducale (p28)

Ghetto Synagogues (p96) Climb to rooftop synagogues on tours run by the Museo Ebraico. (p96)

Scala Contarini del Bovolo A secret spiral staircase in an ancient hidden courtyard. (pictured left; p38)

Best Trade Secrets Revealed

Museo del Vetro Murano kept master glassmaking techniques under wraps for centuries, but here they're on full display. (p135)

Arsenale Workers at Venice's legendary shipyards were sworn to secrecy, but now you can explore the docks during Biennale openings. (p119)

Museo del Merletto Watch lace artisans tat traditional Venetian patterns handed down through centuries. (p141)

Padiglione delle Navi Bodyguards wouldn't let anyone near the *bucintoro* (ducal barge), until now. (p119)

Row Venice Learn to row across lagoon waters standing, like gondoliers do, with regatta champions. (p106)

Best Mysteries in the Attic

Palazzo Mocenigo Head up to the attic closet to discover the kind of shoes a Venetian courtesan wore for streetwalking. (p80)

Palazzo Ducale A tour of the attic prison will reveal just how Casanova escaped captivity while the doge slept downstairs. (p28)

Torre dell'Orologio A tower-top tour will give an up-close look at those bronze bell-ringers who moon the Basilica di San Marco at midnight. (p37)

Best Island Escapes

Drift away on the blue lagoon, and you never know where you'll end up next: at a fiery glass-blowing furnace, an organic farmers market at an island prison, an orphanage designed by Palladio that's now a luxury spa. Venice's lagoon offers not only idyllic island retreats – beachclubs, vineyard lunches and farm-stays – but also outlandish escapes from reality.

MR_ROSS/SHUTTERSTOCK ©

Best Destination Dining

Venissa Ultramodern, ultra-local seafood in an island vineyard. (p144)

Acquastanca Baked goods wedged between glass-blowing studios. (p143)

Trattoria Altanella Authentic Venetian in a vintage trattoria with a flower-hung balcony. (p143)

Locanda Cipriani A wood-beamed dining room and elegant silver service. (p143)

Terra e Acqua Fish risotto aboard a Venetian barge. (p142)

Best Outdoor Attractions

Lido Beaches When temperatures rise, Venice races to the Lido to claim sandy beachfront. (p138)

Torcello Rare lagoon birds swoop lazily past the Byzantine *campanile* on this wild island. (p133)

Venice Kayak Explore the lagoon in peace and quiet under your own steam. (p142)

Vogalonga The regatta race is a fine excuse to laze around Mazzorbo, raising toasts to rowers' health. (pictured above; p146)

Fondazione Giorgio Cini Explore the Borges Labyrinth behind Palladio's cloisters. (p141)

JW Marriott Spa Recline poolside at the Marriott's stunning rooftop spa with Venice at your feet. (p147)

☑ Top Tips

▶ Outer islands are blissfully peaceful in the October–April low season, though some restaurants and shops close.

▶ Ask locals to point out favourite lagoon shorebirds, including white ibis, purple heron and cormorants.

▶ Pick up after island picnics to protect Venice's fragile ecosystem.

Survival Guide

Survival Guide

Before You Go

When to Go
Venice

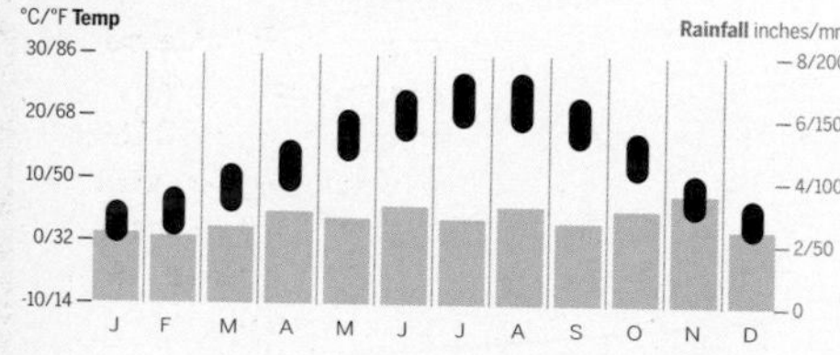

➡ **Spring (Mar–May)** Damp but lovely as ever indoors. Bring an umbrella and enjoy bargain rates – except at Easter.

➡ **Summer (Jun–Aug)** Biennale di Venezia draws the crowds. Temperatures rise and the Rialto is hot, crowded and expensive. Locals escape to the Lido.

➡ **Autumn (Sep–Nov)** After the Venice Film Festival, crowds retreat and rates drop, but the sun still shines.

➡ **Winter (Dec–Feb)** Chilly days with some fog, but nights are sociable, especially during Carnevale.

Book Your Stay

➡ Book ahead for weekend getaways and high-season visits.

➡ Although Venice is a small city, getting around the place can be complicated, so plan where you stay carefully. Easy access to a *vaporetto* (small passenger ferry) stop is key.

➡ Check individual hotel websites for online deals.

➡ Confirm arrival at least 72 hours in advance, or hotels may assume you've changed plans.

➡ For low-season savings of 40% or more, plan visits for November, early December or January to March (except Carnevale). Deals may be found July to August.

Useful Websites

Luxrest Venice (www.luxrest-venice.com) Browse a carefully curated, hand-picked selection of apartments.

Lonely Planet (www.lonelyplanet.com/italy/venice/hotels) Expert author reviews, user feedback, booking engine.

Venice Prestige (www.veniceprestige.com) The crème de la crème of Venetian apartments to rent in aristocratic *palazzi* (mansions).

Views on Venice (www.viewsonvenice.com) A comprehensive selection of apartments picked for their personality, character and view, of course.

Best Budget

Allo Squero (www.allosquero.it) Cannaregio home comforts.

Le Terese (www.leterese.com) Home from home with two architect-styled rooms.

Albergo San Samuele (www.hotelsansamuele.com) Rock-bottom prices right by Palazzo Grassi.

Generator (www.generatorhostels.com) Contemporary hostel cool with canal views.

Best Midrange

Locanda Ca' Le Vele (www.locandalevele.com) Boutique B&B with a heavy dose of Venetian glam.

Venice Halldis Apartments (www.venicehalldisapartments.com) Light, bright, well-priced, Scandi-style modern apartments.

Oltre Il Giardino (www.oltreilgiardino-venezia.com) A romantic garden retreat once home to Alma Mahler's widow.

Residenza de L'Osmarin (www.residenzadelosmarin.com) A true B&B with quilted bedspreads and a slap-up breakfast.

Casa Burano (www.casaburano.it;) Pastel-coloured cottages full of locally crafted furnishings.

Best Top End

Gritti Palace (www.thegrittipalace.com) Grand Canal rooms in a doge's palace.

Al Ponte Antico (www.alponteantico.com) Old-world glamour accompanied by gracious service.

Hotel Palazzo Barbarigo (www.palazzobarbarigo.com) Seductive rooms handily supplied with fainting couches.

Palazzo Abadessa (www.abadessa.com) Frescoed rooms, canal views and a lily-scented garden.

Arriving in Venice

Marco Polo Airport

Venice's main international airport is **Marco Polo Airport** (☎flight information 041 260 92 60; www.veniceairport.it; Via Galileo Gallilei 30/1, Tessera), located in Tessera, 12km east of Mestre.

Inside the airport terminal you'll find ticket offices for water taxis and Alilaguna water bus transfers, an ATM, currency exchange offices, a **left-luggage office** (per item per 24hr €6; ⏰5am-9pm) and a **Vènezia Unica tourist office** (☎041 24 24; www.veneziaunica.it; Arrivals Hall; ⏰8.30am-7pm) where you can pick up pre-ordered travel cards and a map.

Alilaguna Airport Shuttle

There are four water shuttles are operated by **Alilaguna** (☎041 240 17 01; www.alilaguna.it; airport transfer one-way €15) that link the airport with various parts of Venice at a cost of €8 to Murano and €15 to all other landing stages. The ride takes 45 to 90 minutes to reach most destinations. Lines include the following:

Linea Blu (Blue Line) Stops at Lido, San Marco and Dorsoduro.

Linea Rossa (Red Line) Stops at Murano and Lido.

Linea Arancia (Orange Line) Stops at Stazione VeneziaSanta Lucia, Rialto and San Marco via the Grand Canal.

Linea Gialla (Yellow Line) Stops at Murano and Fondamente Nove (Cannaregio).

Bus

Piazzale Roma is the only point within central Venice accessible by bus. *Vaporetto* lines and water taxis depart from Piazzale Roma docks.

ACTV (Azienda del Consorzio Trasporti Veneziano; ☎041 272 21 11; www.actv.it) Bus 5 runs between Marco Polo Airport and Piazzale Roma (€8, 30 minutes, four per hour). A bus+single *vaporetto* ticket costs €14.

ATVO (☎0421 59 46 71; www.atvo.it; Piazzale Roma 497g, Santa Croce; ⏰6.40am-7.45pm) Buses depart from the airport to Piazzale Roma (€8, 25 minutes, every 30 minutes from 8am to midnight).

Water Taxi

Water taxis can be booked at the **Consorzio Motoscafi Venezia** (☎041 240 6712; www.motoscafivenezia.it; ⏰9am-6pm) or **Veneziataxi** (☎information 328 238 9661; www.veneziataxi.it) desks in the arrivals hall, or directly at the dock. Private taxis cost from €110 for up to four passengers and all their luggage.

A shared taxi costs from €25 per person with a €6 surcharge for night-time arrivals. Seats should be booked online at www.venicelink.com. Be aware that shared taxis can wait some time to fill up and have set drop-off points in Venice.

Boats seat a maximum of eight people and can accommodate up to 10 bags.

Taxi

A taxi from the aiport to Piazzale Roma costs €50. From there you can either hop on a *vaporetto* or pick up a **water taxi** (Fondamente Cossetti) at Fondamente Cossetti.

Car

Cars cannot be taken into central Venice.

➡ At Piazzale Roma and Tronchetto parking garages expect to pay from €15 per day.

➡ From Piazzale Roma docks, you can take a *vaporetto* or water taxi.

➡ A **monorail** (APM; www.avmspa.it; Piazzale Roma; per ride €1.50; ⏰7.10am-10.50pm Mon-Sat, 8.10am-9.50pm Sun), also known as the People Mover, connects the Tronchetto parking lots to Piazzale Roma (€1.50 per person).

Stazione Venezia Santa Lucia

All mainland trains terminate in Venice's **Santa Lucia train station** (www.veneziasantalucia.it;

Fondamenta Santa Lucia, Cannaregio), appearing on signs as Ferrovia within Venice. The station has a helpful **tourist office** (041 24 24; www.veneziaunica.it; 7am-9pm; Ferrovia) opposite platform 3 where you can obtain a map and buy *vaporetto* tickets, and a **left-luggage depot** (Deposito Bagagli; 041 78 55 31; 6am-11pm) opposite platform 1.

Vaporetto

Vaporetti connect Santa Lucia train station with all parts of Venice. Lines include the following:

Line 1 Covers the Grand Canal to San Marco and the Lido every 10 minutes.

Line 2 Covers the Grand Canal with fewer stops, returning via Giudecca.

Lines 4.1 & 4.2 Circles Venice's outer perimeter. Convenient for Cannaregio and Castello.

Lines 5.1 & 5.2 Covers the 4.1 and 4.2 route, plus the Lido, with fewer stops..

Line N All-night service stops along Giudecca, the Grand Canal, San Marco and the Lido.

Water Taxi

The water taxi stand is outside the station on Fondamente Cossetti; fares start at €15 and add up quickly at €2 per minute.

Getting Around

Vaporetto

The city's main mode of public transport is the *vaporetto* (small passenger ferry).

- **ACTV** (Azienda del Consorzio Trasporti Veneziano; 041 272 21 11; www.actv.it) runs all public transport in Venice, including all the waterborne public transport.
- Major stops often have two separate docks serving the same *vaporetto* line, heading in opposite directions. Check landing dock signs to make sure you're at the right dock for the direction you want.
- Main lines get full fast, especially between 8am to 10am and 6pm to 8pm. Also, boats can be overcrowded during Carnevale and in peak season.
- Line N offers all-night local service covering Giudecca, the Grand Canal, San Marco and the Lido (11.30am to 4am, about every 40 minutes).
- Inter-island ferry services to Murano, Torcello, the Lido and other lagoon islands are usually provided on larger *motonave* (big inter-island *vaporetti*).

Tickets & Passes

Vènezia Unica (041 24 24; www.veneziaunica.it) is the main ticket seller, and you can purchase *vaporetti* tickets at booths at most landing stations. Tickets and multiday passes can also be prepurchased online.

- A one-way tickets cost €7.50.
- If you're going to be using the *vaporetto* frequently (more than three trips), consider a Travel Card, which allows unlimited travel in set time periods.
- Always validate your ticket at yellow dockside machines at first usage. If you're caught without

a valid ticket you'll be fined €59 (plus the €7.50 fare) on the spot.

➡ People aged 14 to 29 holding a Rolling Venice card can get a three-day ticket for €20 at tourist offices.

Gondola

Gondolas cluster at *stazi* (stops) along the Grand Canal and near major monuments and tourist hot spots, but you can also book a pick-up by calling **Ente Gondola** (☎041 528 50 75; www.gondolavenezia.it).

➡ Rates are €80 for 40 minutes (it's €100 for 35 minutes from 7pm to 8am), not including any songs or tips. Additional time after that is charged in 20-minute increments (day/night €40/50).

➡ **Gondolas 4 All** (☎328 2431382; www.gondolas4all.com; Fondamente Cossetti, Santa Croce), supported by the Gondoliers Association, offers gondola rides to wheelchair users in a specially adapted gondola. Embarkation is from a wheelchair-accessible pier at Piazzale Roma.

Traghetto

A *traghetto* is the gondola service locals use to cross the Grand Canal between bridges (€2, 9am to 6pm, some routes to noon).

Water Taxi

Licensed water taxis offer stylish transport in sleek teak boats.

➡ Fares start at €15 plus €2 per minute, €5 extra if the water taxi is called to your hotel. There's a €10 surcharge for night trips (10pm to 6am), a €5 surcharge for additional luggage (above five pieces) and a €10 surcharge for each extra passenger above the first four. Tipping isn't required.

➡ If you order a water taxi through your hotel or a travel agent, you will be subject to a surcharge.

➡ Even if you're in a hurry, please don't be tempted to encourage your taxi driver to speed – *motoschiaffi* (wake from motorboats) expose Venice's ancient foundations to degradation.

Bicycle

Cycling is banned in central Venice.

On the Lido, cycling is a pleasant way to reach distant beaches.

Lido on Bike (☎041 526 80 19; www.lidoonbike.it; Gran Viale Santa Maria Elisabetta 21b, Lido; bicycle rental per 90min/day €5/9; 🕘9am-7pm summer; ⛴Lido SME) is located near the *vaporetto* (small passenger ferry) stop; ID is required for rental.

Essential Information

Business Hours

The hours listed here are a general guide; individual establishments can vary.

Banks 8.30am to 1.30pm and 3.30pm to 5.30pm Monday to Friday; some open Saturday mornings.

Restaurants Noon to 2.30pm and 7pm to 10pm.

Shops 10am to 1pm and 3.30pm to 7pm (or 4pm

to 7.30pm) Monday to Saturday.

Discount Cards

The tourist information portal, **Vènezia Unica** (☎041 24 24; www.venezia unica.it), brings together a range of discount passes and services and enables you to tailor them to your needs and pre-purchase online. Services and passes on offer include the following:

- land and water transfers to the airport and cruise terminal
- ACTV Travel Cards
- museum and church passes
- select parking
- citywide wi-fi
- prepaid access to public toilets

If purchasing online you need to print out your voucher displaying your reservation number (PNR) and carry it with you, then simply present it at the various attractions for admission or access.

To use public transport, you will need to obtain a free card (you will need your PNR code from your booking to do this), which is then 'loaded' with credit. You can obtain this at the ACTV ticket machines at Marco Polo Airport, ticket desks at *vaporetto* stops and Vènezia Unica offices.

Chorus Pass

Offers single entry to 16 churches (adult/student under 29 years €12/8). Valid for one year. Buy at participating churches.

Civic Museum Pass

This pass (adult/reduced €24/18) is valid for six months and covers single entry to 11 civic museums, including Palazzo Ducale and the Museo Correr. Available from any civic museum or the tourist office.

City Pass

City passes are available from Vènezia Unica (☎041 24 24; www.venezia unica.it). The most useful include:

City Pass (adult/junior €39.90/29.90) Valid for seven days, offering entrance to 11 civic museums, 16 Chorus churches, the Fondazione Querini Stampalia and the Museo Ebraico (Jewish Museum). It also includes free admission to the casino.

St Mark's City Pass (€27.90) A reduced version of the City Pass allowing entry to the three civic museums on Piazza San Marco, plus three churches on the Chorus Circuit and the Fondazione Querini Stampalia.

Other Combined Museum Tickets

- A combined ticket to Ca' d'Oro and Palazzo Grimani costs adult/student/senior €10/8/free and is valid for three months.
- A combined ticket to the Palazzo Grassi and Punta della Dogana costs adult/reduced €18/15.

Rolling Venice Card

Visitors aged 6 to 29 years should pick up the €6 Rolling Venice card (from tourist offices and most ACTV public transport ticket points), entitling purchase of a 72-hour public transport pass (€22) and discounts on airport transfers, museums, monuments and cultural events.

Electricity

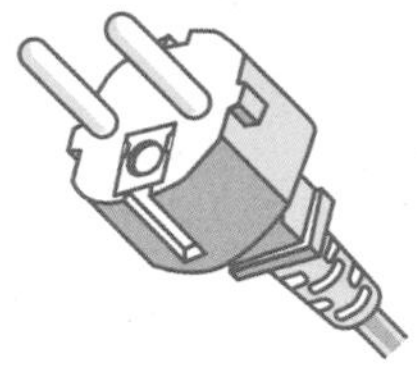

Type F
230V/50Hz

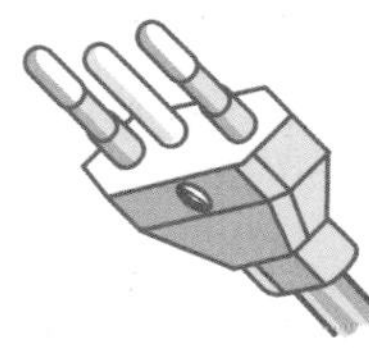

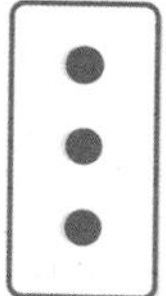

Type L
220V/50Hz

Money

ATMs Widely available

Credit cards Accepted at most hotels, B&Bs and shops.

Money changers At banks, airport and some hotels; you'll need ID.

Tipping Ten per cent optional for good restaurant, hotel and gondola services.

Public Holidays

Holidays that may affect opening hours and transit schedules:

Capodanno/Anno Nuovo (New Year's Day) 1 January

Epifania/Befana (Epiphany) 6 January

Pasquetta/Lunedì dell'Angelo (Easter Monday) March/April

Giorno della Liberazione (Liberation Day) 25 April

Festa del Lavoro (Labour Day) 1 May

Festa della Repubblica (Republic Day) 2 June

Ferragosto (Feast of the Assumption) 15 August

Ognissanti (All Saints' Day) 1 November

Immaculata Concezione (Feast of the Immaculate Conception) 8 December

Natale (Christmas Day) 25 December

Festa di Santo Stefano (Boxing Day) 26 December

Safe Travel

Precautions Mind your step on slippery canal banks, especially after rains. Watch out for petty theft around Venice's train station.

Children Few canal banks and bridges have railings, and most Gothic palaces have lots of stairs.

Rising water Flooding in low-lying areas is a regular occurrence in Venice. See p110 for more information.

Telephone

Mobile Phones

GSM and tri-band phones can be used in Italy with a local SIM card.

Area Codes

The dialling code for Italy is ☎39. The city code for Venice is ☎041. The city code is an integral part of the number and must always be dialled. Toll-free (free-phone) numbers are known as *numeri verdi* and usually start with ☎800.

International Calls

The cheapest options for calling internationally are free or low-cost computer programs such as Skype, FaceTime and Viber, cut-rate call centres or international dialling cards, which are sold at news-stands and tobacconists. All of these offer cheaper calls than the Telecom payphones.

If you're calling an international number from an Italian phone, you must dial ☎00 to get an international line, then the relevant country and city codes, followed by the telephone number.

To call Venice from abroad, call the international access number for Italy (☎011 in the United States, ☎00 from most other countries), Italy's country code ☎39, then the Venice area code ☎041, followed by the telephone number.

Dos & Don'ts

➡ Do keep right along narrow lanes and let people pass on the left.

➡ Don't linger on small bridges taking photographs at lunchtime and 3pm during the school run. And avoid selfie sticks which threaten to poke passers-by in the eye.

➡ Do offer help to people struggling with strollers or bags on bridges.

➡ Don't push. Allow passengers to disembark before boarding boats. Pay attention to calls of *'Permesso!'* (Pardon!) as people try to exit busy boats.

Toilets

Public toilets Available near tourist attractions (€1.50) and open from 7am to 7pm.

Bars and cafes For customers only. Look before you sit: even in women's bathrooms, some toilets don't have seats.

Museums This is your best option – where available.

Tourist Information

Vènezia Unica (☎041 24 24; www.veneziaunica.it) runs all tourist information services and offices in Venice. It provides information on sights, itineraries, day trips, transport, special events, shows and temporary exhibitions. Discount passes can be prebooked on its website.

Find offices at Marco Polo Airport, Santa Lucia train station and on Piazza San Marco.

Travellers with Disabilities

With nearly 400 footbridges and endless stairs, Venice is not an easy place for travellers with disabilities.

➡ *Vaporetti* are the most effective way to access sites and avoid bridges. Passengers in wheelchairs travel for just €1.50, while their companion travels free.

➡ The **Disabled Assistance Office** (Sala Blu; ☎800 906 060; Stazione Venezia Santa Lucia;

7am-9.30pm) is located at platform 4 in Venice's Santa Lucia train station.

➡ The most accessible tourist office is the one off Piazza San Marco.

➡ With ID, most museums offer free or discounted admission to disabled visitors with one companion.

➡ A printable *Accessible Venice* map is available from the tourist office. The map delimits the area around each water-bus stop that can be accessed without crossing a bridge. In addition, the website provides 12 'barrier-free' itineraries, which can be downloaded.

➡ Of the other islands, Murano, Burano, the Lido and Torcello are all fairly easy to access.

➡ Download Lonely Planet's free Accessible Travel guide from http://lptravel.to/AccessibleTravel.

Organisations

Accessible Italy (www.accessibleitaly.com) A San Marino–based company that specialises in holiday services for people with disabilities. This is the best port of call.

L'Altra Venezia (www.laltravenezia.it; walking tours €70, thematic tours from €200, boat tours from €480) Offers lagoon tours in specially adapted boats that can accommodate multiple wheelchairs and up to 10 people.

Visas

Not required for EU citizens. Nationals of Australia, Brazil, Canada, Japan, New Zealand and the USA do not need visas for visits of up to 90 days. For more information, visit the Italian foreign ministry website (www.esteri.it).

Language

Regional dialects are an important part of identity in many parts of Italy, but you'll have no trouble being understood in Venice or anywhere else in the country if you stick to standard Italian, which is what we've also used in this chapter.

The sounds used in spoken Italian can all be found in English. If you read our pronunciation guides as if they were English, you'll be understood. The stressed syllables are indicated with italics. Note that *ai* is pronounced as in 'aisle', *ay* as in 'say', *ow* as in 'how', *dz* as the 'ds' in 'lids', and that *r* is a strong and rolled sound.

To enhance your trip with a phrasebook, visit **lonelyplanet.com**. Lonely Planet iPhone phrasebooks are available through the Apple App store.

Basics

Hello.
Buongiorno. bwon·*jor*·no

Goodbye.
Arrivederci. a·ree·ve·*der*·chee

How are you?
Come sta? *ko*·me sta

Fine. And you?
Bene. E Lei? *be*·ne e lay

Please.
Per favore. per fa·*vo*·re

Thank you.
Grazie. *gra*·tsye

Excuse me.
Mi scusi. mee *skoo*·zee

Sorry.
Mi dispiace. mee dees·*pya*·che

Yes./No.
Sì./No. see/no

I don't understand.
Non capisco. non ka·*pee*·sko

Do you speak English?
Parla inglese? *par*·la een·*gle*·ze

Eating & Drinking

I'd like ...	*Vorrei ...*	vo·*ray* ...
a coffee	*un caffè*	oon ka·*fe*
a table	*un tavolo*	oon *ta*·vo·lo
the menu	*il menù*	eel me·*noo*
two beers	*due birre*	*doo*·e *bee*·re

What would you recommend?
Cosa mi consiglia? *ko*·za mee kon·*see*·lya

Enjoy the meal!
Buon appetito! bwon a·pe·*tee*·to

That was delicious!
Era squisito! *e*·ra skwee·*zee*·to

Cheers!
Salute! sa·*loo*·te

Can you bring me the bill, please?
Mi porta il conto, per favore? mee *por*·ta eel *kon*·to per fa·*vo*·re

Shopping

I'd like to buy ...
Vorrei comprare ... vo·*ray* kom·*pra*·re ...

I'm just looking.
Sto solo guardando. sto *so*·lo gwar·*dan*·do

How much is this?
Quanto costa questto? — kwan·to kos·ta kwe·sto

It's too expensive.
È troppo caro/cara. (m/f) — e tro·po ka·ro/ka·ra

Emergencies

Help!
Aiuto! — a·yoo·to

Call the police!
Chiami la polizia! — kya·mee la po·lee·tsee·a

Call a doctor!
Chiami un medico! — kya·mee oon me·dee·ko

I'm sick.
Mi sento male. — mee sen·to ma·le

I'm lost.
Mi sono perso/persa. (m/f) — mee so·no per·so/per·sa

Where are the toilets?
Dove sono i gabinetti? — do·ve so·no ee ga·bee·ne·tee

Time & Numbers

What time is it?
Che ora è? — ke o·ra e

It's (two) o'clock.
Sono le (due). — so·no le (doo·e)

morning	*mattina*	ma·tee·na
afternoon	*pomeriggio*	po·me·ree·jo
evening	*sera*	se·ra
yesterday	*ieri*	ye·ree
today	*oggi*	o·jee
tomorrow	*domani*	do·ma·nee

1	*uno*	oo·no
2	*due*	doo·e
3	*tre*	tre
4	*quattro*	kwa·tro
5	*cinque*	cheen·kwe
6	*sei*	say
7	*sette*	se·te
8	*otto*	o·to
9	*nove*	no·ve
10	*dieci*	dye·chee
100	*cento*	chen·to
1000	*mille*	mee·le

Transport & Directions

Where's ...?
Dov'è ...? — do·ve ...

What's the address?
Qual'è l'indirizzo? — kwa·le leen·dee·ree·tso

Can you show me (on the map)?
Può mostrarmi (sulla pianta)? — pwo mos·trar·mee (soo·la pyan·ta)

At what time does the ... leave?
A che ora parte ...? — a ke o·ra par·te ...

Does it stop at ...?
Si ferma a ...? — see fer·ma a ...

How do I get there?
Come ci si arriva? — ko·me chee see a·ree·va

bus	*autobus*	ow·to·boos
ticket	*biglietto*	bee·lye·to
timetable	*orario*	o·ra·ryo
train	*il treno*	eel tre·no

Behind the Scenes

Send Us Your Feedback

We love to hear from travellers – your comments help make our books better. We read every word, and we guarantee that your feedback goes straight to the authors. Visit **lonelyplanet.com/contact** to submit your updates and suggestions.

Note: We may edit, reproduce and incorporate your comments in Lonely Planet products such as guidebooks, websites and digital products, so let us know if you don't want your comments reproduced or your name acknowledged. For a copy of our privacy policy visit lonelyplanet.com/privacy.

Paula's Thanks

Grazie mille to all the fun and fashionable Venetians who spilled the beans on their remarkable city: Paola dalla Valentina, Costanza Cecchini, Sara Porro, Lucia Cattaneo, Monica Cesarato, Francesca Giubilei, Luca Berta, Marco Secchi and Nan McElroy. Thanks to Anna Tyler for all the support. Finally, much love to Rob for sharing the beauty of the *bel paese*.

Peter's Thanks

It's not hard to find willing volunteers to keep you company on an extended research assignment in Venice, especially when it coincides with Carnevale. Many thanks to my Venice crew of Christine Henderson, Hamish Blennerhassett and Sarah Welch for much masked fun and many good meals. Special thanks to Christine for the unpaid but much appreciated translation services.

Acknowledgements

Cover photograph: scene with traditional gondola and canal in Venice, Italy. canadastock/Shutterstock ©

Contents photograph: Palazzo Ducale, valentinrussanov/Getty Images ©

This Book

This 4th edition of Lonely Planet's *Pocket Venice* guidebook was researched and written by Paula Hardy and Peter Dragicevich. The previous two editions were written by Alison Bing. This guidebook was produced by the following:

Destination Editor Anna Tyler

Product Editors Vicky Smith, Anne Mason

Regional Senior Cartographer Anthony Phelan

Book Designer Clara Monitto

Assisting Editors Imogen Bannister, Gabby Innes, Monique Perrin, Gabrielle Stefanos, Fionn Twomey

Cartographer Valentina Kremenchutskaya

Cover Researcher Naomi Parker

Thanks to Sasha Drew, Hannah Kempster, Jane Lanigan, Jorge Lázaro, Karl Palmer, Kate Mathews, Susan North

Index

See also separate subindexes for:
- Eating p189
- Drinking p189
- Entertainment p190
- Shopping p190

Sights p000
Map Pages **p000**

Sights p000
Map Pages **p000**

Eating

Drinking

Entertainment

Shopping

Sights p000
Map Pages **p000**